From Our Hearts to Yours

REFLECTIONS FROM DIANA HAGEE,
JUDY JACOBS, LISA BEVERE
AND MANY MORE

From
OUR HEARTS
to
YOURS

Charisma
HOUSE
A STRANG COMPANY

Most Strang Communications/Charisma House/Siloam/Excel Books/FrontLine/Realms products are available at special quantity discounts for bulk purchase for sales promotions, premiums, fund-raising, and educational needs. For details, write Strang Communications/Charisma House/Siloam/Excel Books/FrontLine/Realms, 600 Rinehart Road, Lake Mary, Florida 32746, or telephone (407) 333-0600.

From Our Hearts to Yours edited by Charisma House
Published by Charisma House
A Strang Company
600 Rinehart Road
Lake Mary, Florida 32746
www.charismahouse.com

Cover Designer: Jerry Pomales
Executive Design Director: Bill Johnson

Library of Congress Cataloging-in-Publication Data:

From our hearts to yours / edited by Charisma House.

    p. cm.
  ISBN 978-1-59979-229-3
  1. Christian women--Religious life. 2. Spirituality. 3. Spiritual life--Christianity. 4. Christian life. I. Charisma House.

  BV4527.F758 2008
  242'.643--dc22

                                            2007032371

First Edition

08 09 10 11 12 — 9 8 7 6 5 4 3 2 1
Printed in the United States of America

From
OUR HEARTS
to YOURS

Amazing experiences and heartfelt insights
from the hearts of women revealing
God's love for you

CONTENTS

SECTION 2—BECOMING A WOMAN OF LOVE

SECTION 3—EXPERIENCING LIFE WITH OTHERS

INTRODUCTION

THERE IS NO GREATER FEELING IN THE WORLD THAN THE feeling of being loved—unconditionally, irrevocably, eternally loved! And there is only one source for a love like that. Our Father God Himself has whispered to each of us:

> Yes, I have loved you with an everlasting love; therefore with lovingkindness I have drawn you. Again I will build you, and you shall be rebuilt.
>
> —Jeremiah 31:3–4, NKJV

This book is being presented by the editors of Charisma House to you for those moments when you need to be reassured once again of that unwavering, eternal love of God. It's for those times when you need to be built—or rebuilt—and all the moments in between.

We wanted you to be encompassed by the reality of that love as you live each day of your life. We have chosen to concentrate on three vital areas of a woman's life.

- We want you to increase in your ability to trust your heavenly Father's love in every circumstance of life—good and bad.

- We want you to recognize the ways that your heavenly Father's love can help you to become a woman of love from the inside out.

- And we want God's love to give you the examples and principles you need to express His love to others as you experience life with them.

So find a cozy spot to curl up with this special book written just for you, and share in the stories, examples, and teachings from other women just like you—women who know God loves them supremely and who are trying to show that love to others more effectively through their own lives.

> Beloved, let us love one another, for love is of God; and everyone who loves is born of God and knows God. He who does not love does not know God, for God is love. In this the love of God was manifested toward us, that God has sent His only begotten Son into the world, that we might live through Him. In this is love, not that we loved God, but that He loved us and sent His Son to be the propitiation for our sins. Beloved, if God so loved us, we also ought to love one another.
>
> —1 John 4:7–11, NKJV

—From the Editors of Charisma House

SECTION ONE

TRUSTING *the* FATHER'S LOVE *for* YOU

ONE

LEARNING *to* STAND STRONG

by
Judy Jacobs

WHAT DO YOU DO WHEN YOU HAVE DONE IT ALL? You stand.

For that matter, what do you do the whole time you're actively "doing"—praying, fasting, fighting, proclaiming, and so on? You stand.

You stand as tall as you can, with your feet flat on the ground, strong in your faith. You keep your mouth open with praise and your eyes open for God to show you the supernatural. You keep your hands raised to give Him praise. You keep your heart pure.

You don't sit down. You don't lie down. You don't run off anxiously to another prayer meeting. You don't call your mama. You don't dial 911. You just simply stand.

Standing strong depends on more than how sturdy your legs are. Standing strong means you are strong in your spirit.

When you are strong in your spirit, you can stand tall (with confidence) and stand long (with perseverance) because you're drawing from a core of strength in your spirit. You have a full reservoir of spiritual strength that comes from God.

Don't get confused about it—your inner strength is not the same as being a tough person, someone who has been hardened by life experiences. To stand strong, you do not (necessarily) need a degree from the School of Hard Knocks. You don't stand strong in the way I'm talking about just because you have German, African, or Native American heritage. It's not because you happened to grow up in New York City or in Montana on the ranch that your granddaddy homesteaded, and it's not because your mean big brother used to beat you up.

You stand strong in your spirit because you are filled with God's Spirit. But you are only strong in your spirit because you are, in and of yourself, weak. Paul said, "When I am weak, then I am strong" (2 Cor. 12:10, NKJV). You have such limited power of your own that you need to keep asking for God's Spirit to fill you up. And that keeps you growing stronger all the time.

To stand strong in God's Spirit is the only way to truly stand strong. All the other kinds of strong standing are like mere shadows of the real thing. It is a level of stamina that believes God regardless. It is simply knowing who God is, knowing that you can trust Him to be who He says He is, trusting Him to do what He says He will do.

It's not just for our own sakes that we get saved. It's not just for pie-in-the-sky by-and-by. It's for other people's sakes. It's for your sons and daughters. It's for your husband or wife. It's for your relatives. It's for your friends, neighbors, and co-workers—for anybody who crosses your path. You're part of the defending army, and you're armed. Stand strong in your full armor of God, and you'll be ready when people need to hook onto you and Jesus. Stand strong in the grace of Jesus, all of the time.

Judy Jacobs, *Stand Strong* (Lake Mary, FL, Charisma House, 2007), viii, 17–18, 30.

TWO

The ONLY PERFECT LOVE

by

Lisa Bevere

THE LORD LOVES WOMEN. CERTAINLY HE ALWAYS HAS. Jesus befriended a woman who was shunned by her entire community. He allowed a scandalous woman to anoint Him.

When Mary sat worshiping at His feet, He wouldn't permit the busy Martha to remove her. Even as He died on the cross, He was thinking of a woman.

John 19:26–27 recounts one of His final thoughts: "When Jesus saw his mother there, and the disciple whom he loved standing nearby, he said to his mother, 'Dear woman, here is your son,' and to the disciple, 'Here is your mother.' From that time on, this disciple took her into his home" (NIV).

His beloved mother wasn't the only woman who crossed His mind in that moment of unbearable pain. He was also thinking of you and me. He couldn't imagine eternity without us, so He willingly surrendered His earthly life in our place.

I remember the day—even the hour—when I discovered His irresistible love. What man had ever shown me such faithfulness and dedication? Who had ever spoken so tenderly? When had I ever been forgiven so completely? In exchange for my broken body and empty heart, He offered me everything.

Before that moment, my life had been a series of shallow gasps. But when His love flooded my being, I was finally able to take a deep breath. Jesus is the only one from whom every woman—single or married—can honestly find her worth. God never meant for women to seek their value from men. He meant for us to look to Him.

If we're honest with ourselves, we'll find that we inadvertently declare man to be our "god" on multiple levels. We express this through how we spend our money, our time, and our energy. Advertisers prey upon our desire to be in a relationship by suggesting that if we look and dress like "this" (the desirable woman) we'll get "that" (the man of our dreams).

In a sense, we're invited to costume balls where only the perfect and beautiful ultimately win. Think Cinderella. She had the ideal dress, hair, accessories, and even shoes. The underlying message is this: the perfect Prince Charming equals the perfect life. But there's no such thing as a perfect man (or woman). There's only a perfect God.

We are designed to find our ultimate purpose in God alone. There are promises made to us that only He can keep.

Seek Your True Source

Favor with God is realized in secret. Alone with Him, our motives are weighed and revealed. In His presence all expectations and disappointments are laid to rest. There, we're embraced for who we are, not for what we do. This is reality. Who we are with Him is much more important than anything we might accomplish for Him in the public arena.

Sometimes I run to the safety of His presence because I'm

afraid and I've lost perspective. There, I'm reminded of His truth: "Fear of man will prove to be a snare, but whoever trusts in the LORD is kept safe" (Prov. 29:25, NIV). And, "In God I trust; I will not be afraid. What can man do to me?" (Ps. 56:11, NIV). The psalmist raises a good question. People will come against us, but what can they actually do to us if we trust in God? If we believe God when He tells us that He holds our life in His hands, then we'll find ourselves unafraid of the threats of man.

If we're walking this earth, we will be misunderstood, misjudged, misrepresented, and mistaken by friends and enemies alike—but never by God. "It is better to trust in the LORD than to put confidence in man" (Ps. 118:8, NKJV). This isn't an admonishment to distrust people, but it's a reminder of where to place your trust. It's better to totally surrender to God's mercy and fairness than to even think of relying on people.

The only way to trust God more is to know Him better. He's unchanging and righteous. He's truth. His honor is above question, and His power is limitless. And, thank goodness, He is altogether different than us.

Lisa Bevere, "The Only Perfect Love," *SpiritLed Woman*, April/May 2006, 26–29

THREE

JESUS KNOWS WHERE YOU LIVE

by

Joy Dawson

WHEN WE ARE TEMPTED TO THINK GOD HAS FORGOTTEN our address, we need to meditate on the following scriptures:

> "I have told you that I am He. Therefore, if you seek Me, let these go their way," that the saying might be fulfilled which He spoke, "Of those whom You gave Me I have lost none."
> —John 18:8–9, NKJV

These protective words were spoken when Jesus was about to be led away, prior to His crucifixion. Jesus was fulfilling His promise to His friends then and to His friends now: "I will never leave you nor forsake you" (Heb. 13:5, NKJV).

Jesus's concerned love was never more evidenced than when He was speaking about how we should relate to children. Listen to His gentleness in Isaiah 40:11: "He will feed His flock like a shepherd; He will gather the lambs with His arm, and carry them in His bosom, and gently lead those who are with young" (NKJV). Listen to the way Jesus identified Himself and His Father God with them:

> Then He took a little child and set him in the midst of them. And when He had taken him in His arms, He said to them, "Whoever receives one of these little children in My name receives Me; and whoever receives Me, receives not Me but Him who sent Me."
>
> —Mark 9:36–37, NKJV

This statement infers that to reject a child is rejecting Jesus. This is emphasized again when Jesus rebuked His disciples for trying to keep people from bringing children to Him: "But when Jesus saw it, He was greatly displeased and said to them, 'Let the little children come to Me, and do not forbid them; for of such is the kingdom of God'" (Mark 10:14, NKJV). We can often measure our Christlikeness by the value we place on children and how we treat them.

I love to think about Jesus's pursuing love in friendship from the story of the man whom He healed from blindness on the Sabbath day. After the Pharisees had belittled and rejected Jesus and the man, the Bible says that Jesus went and looked for him until He found him in the temple. Then Jesus revealed Himself more fully to him. What a loving friend.

Perhaps the most poignant picture of Jesus's caring love as a friend would be when He was hanging on the cross in unspeakable agony. He looked down at His devoted mother, Mary, understanding the intensity of her grief-stricken heart. He looked at John, the closest male gift of friendship His Father had given Him. Jesus understood the depth of John's suffering and pain. Jesus knew how desperately these two would need each other in the coming days. And in His infinitely loving, caring, and concerned heart for their needs, He gave them as permanent gifts of friendships to share the same home together. Jesus, our compassionate friend, knows exactly what our friendship needs are for every stage of our lives, and He has a perfect plan to meet them.

Perhaps you're widowed like Mary, or are concerned how you would cope on your own if you became widowed. Whatever it is that concerns us in relation to our being cared for, we can take comfort in the certainty of one thing. Jesus said that He's looking out for and watching over the needs of each little sparrow—and that you and I are of much more value and concern to Him than these little birds. Have you ever seen a worried bird?

If you're still worried about your future, be at rest as you read these wonderful words about the Lord Jesus as a friend: "Having loved His own who were in the world, He loved them *to the end*" (John 13:1, NKJV, emphasis added). Jesus assures us that He will look after us right to the end of our lives, as we keep worshiping Him, obeying Him, believing Him, and trusting Him.

Joy Dawson, *Jesus the Model* (Lake Mary, FL: Charisma House, 2007), 81–84.

FOUR

GOD HAS *the* INSTRUCTION MANUAL *for* LIFE

by

Cathy Lechner

HAVE YOU EVER FELT AS THOUGH YOU NEED AN INSTRUCtion manual for life? Just about the time you think you have it figured out, along comes a curve ball, and you end up wandering about in the wilderness. God brings you into the wilderness to humble you and to show you what is in your heart. Will you do the will of God in the wilderness?

The entire kingdom of God can be summed up by the A to Z principle. Point A is where we begin, where we start our Christian walk; point Z is where all the promises come to pass.

At point A, the Spirit of the Lord says to us, "Daughter, do you want to see your destiny? Do you want Me to speak and show you what I have for you?" Our reply is, "Yes, God. I want it! I want to see it!"

He tells us, "Enter and possess your promise." We say, "All right, I can do that."

At point C, we find we're right in the middle in the valley

of the shadow that looks like death. But we press on to points E, F, and G and say, "Lord, what's going on?"

We start doing warfare. We bind everything. I used to make a religion out of binding things. "I bind you to the third and fourth degree and the fifth and seventh level."

Then we reach points L and M. That's when we say, "Oh Jesus, just kill me. Take me home. I can't take it anymore. If it weren't for my children I could just die right now."

Jesus doesn't kill you, because the object is not to get you to heaven but to get heaven in you. If God wanted you in heaven, as soon as you got saved He would have given your pastor a gun and, *bang!* He would have punched your ticket and sent you to heaven.

You press on until you get to R and S, and you think, "Where's that person who gave me this word? I want their name and number. I don't want any more prophecies."

Finally, we get to X and Y. That's where we can say, "Lord, if You take me in and bring Your promise to pass, I'll praise Your name. If You don't bring it to pass, I'll praise Your name. All I want is to glorify You." And then *boom!* The Spirit of God takes us right into Z.

You may be thinking, "Cathy, if I had known that back at point A, I'd have said, 'I'll praise Your name whether You bring me in or not.'"

But God doesn't do that, because He knows you need to go through A to Y so He can work the character of His Son in you. The person who goes into the wilderness is not the same person who comes out. The wilderness experience transforms.

Cathy Lechner, *I'm Trying to Sit at His Feet, but Who's Going to Cook Dinner?* (Lake Mary, FL: Charisma House, 1995), 64–66.

FIVE

SAY YES *to* GOD'S PROMISES

by

Heidi Baker

HAVE YOU EVER HAD A PROPHETIC WORD FROM GOD THAT was beyond what you could ask, think, or imagine? God loves to blow up our little boxes. What price did you pay before the word came to pass?

The reason I ask is because many Christians eagerly desire the prophetic without having a clue what it will cost them.

How much will it cost to follow Jesus? Everything. Just ask Mary. Luke 1:26 tells us, "God sent the angel Gabriel to Nazareth, a town in Galilee, to a virgin pledged to be married to a man named Joseph, a descendant of David. The virgin's name was Mary. The angel went to her and said, 'Greetings, you who are highly favored!'" (NIV).

What would you do if an angel showed up on your doorstep, proclaiming, "Greetings, you are highly favored"? Would you jump up and down saying: "Hooray! God is here"?

I don't think so. Perhaps you would fall on your face. You would tremble before the Lord. You would be wrecked, completely undone, ruined forever. That was Mary's response. When the angel appeared, she was terrified, not overjoyed.

Luke 1:29–30 says, "Mary was greatly troubled at [his] words and wondered what kind of greeting this might be'" (NIV).

I can identify with Mary. You see, when I was sixteen years old, I had a radical visitation from God. I had been a Christian only five months when God spoke audibly to me. He told me that I would be a missionary and minister. I was forever transformed. I alternated between sobbing and laughing. I began running after that prophetic vision with all my heart. Thirty years later, I'm still chasing after my God dreams.

I love running into the darkest of the darkness to see His glorious light shine forth. I could not imagine doing anything but laying down my life for love's sake. Why? Because He ruined me with His love. I promised Jesus, "I will do whatever You ask no matter the cost."

After that experience, I followed the Word and began to preach the gospel. As a sixteen-year-old girl, I first preached to Alzheimer's patients, drug addicts, and anyone who would listen. Eventually I preached in Asia and England and all over the world. Today I live and minister in Mozambique, Africa.

When God visited me and promised me something so much beyond myself, I had a choice. At the time, I had never even heard of women preachers. But I chose not to doubt and look to the natural. I believed His word. He told me to preach, so I preached. That word has cost me everything, but it is my greatest joy and privilege.

As I have laid my little life down, I am now watching a nation run to Him. I have been shot at, thrown in jail, slandered, stabbed, diagnosed then healed of many terminal illnesses, and experienced trials too great to tell. My family has been without food, water, or support. We have been beaten, threatened, and had all manner of evil spoken against us. But this is nothing compared to the all-surpassing joy of knowing Him.

Jesus is my model and hero. He spared nothing and gave up the riches of heaven as the ultimate missionary. He came down to Earth just for us. Jesus was love incarnate. Every day He poured forth limitless, unceasing love to each and every person in front of Him no matter the pain of it all.

Now our job on Earth is to follow His example and love no matter the cost. No matter how impossible a prophetic word seems, we must follow the Lamb who was slain, to give Him the just reward for His sufferings. God challenges me every day to remain in love no matter the trials and tribulations.

God is looking for yielded vessels. He is looking for people who will say: "Yes, Lord. Here I am. I don't care what it costs. Be it unto me."

Is there a yes in you for God? Is there a yes in you for the promise that He wants to place inside you? Mary's life was never the same after her visitation from God. It cost her everything, beginning with her reputation and ending with the sight of her beloved Son dying on a cross. Yet listen to her response: "My soul magnifies the Lord, and my spirit has rejoiced in God my Savior. For He has regarded the lowly state of His maidservant; for behold, henceforth all generations will call me blessed" (Luke 1:46–48, NKJV).

Like Mary, we too can rejoice in our great God. He is our portion and our exceedingly great reward. He loves us, and He wants to birth His great promises within us. All we need to do is say, "Yes, Lord!"

Heidi Baker, "Say Yes to God's Promises," *SpiritLed Woman*, December/January 2007, 16–19.

SIX

PRAYER *and* FAITH MAKE *a* BEAUTIFUL SYMPHONY

by

Judy Jacobs

THERE IS NOTHING MORE EFFECTIVE ON THE FACE OF THIS earth than the power of prayer and the far-reaching hand of faith. Prayer and faith fit together like a beautiful symphony of orchestral music. Never underestimate them, for they have altered the course of nature, changed the laws of the universe, and have even influenced and changed the mind of God.

Having grown up in a home that was inundated with prayer, I understand its power. Mentored in a life of prayer by godly parents, family, and the covering of a home church, I have been able to see the impossible come to pass through the simple eyes of faith, and I will forever be affected.

I also understand what it means to tarry in prayer and wait before God in anticipation of seeing prayers answered. I remember as a small child falling asleep in the pews, and as I approached my adolescent years, I really didn't look forward to being in those "all-night prayer meetings." However, as I began to mature in stature and in the Lord, I saw the necessity of persevering and tarrying in prayer. One thing that I realized early on in life was that prayer and faith really work!

We are being exposed to a lot of talk about God, prayer, and faith now that we are living in this pressurized, fear-craven, terrorist-stricken society. We turn on our television and don't know what to expect from week to week. What terror-alert color code will our nation be under today? What will happen in the Middle East? Where will the terrorists strike next? More than ever before, it is "politically correct" to have some belief system of God or some form of God. It is even more acceptable to pray, as long as you are praying what the world deems as a nonthreatening prayer or that which stays within the parameters of what is acceptable, which is no mention of Jesus Christ, the blood, or the cross.

This world is drowning in a sea of fear, hopelessness, depravity, promiscuity, and godlessness. They are looking for someone to throw them a life preserver, anyone who just looks like they know how to stay afloat in this sea called life. The church has to be wide-awake to the hurting, the forgotten, the lost, the lonely, and the abandoned. The scheme of the enemy is "to steal, kill, and destroy" this generation that has a promise of ushering in the return of our Lord and Savior, Jesus Christ.

Along with this recognition of our enemy, we must be fully convinced about our faith and our God. We must trust in the infallible Word of the living God, and the only God worth knowing, loving, and serving is Jehovah God, the creator and sustainer of everything that exists.

Judy Jacobs, *Take It By Force!* (Lake Mary, FL: Charisma House, 2005), 1, 3–4.

SEVEN

WORDS WORTH AGREEING WITH

by

Cindy Trimm

WHEN YOU READ ONE OF GOD'S PROMISES TO YOU IN THE Bible, what is your first thought? Do you think, "What a wonderful promise! Of course, that is not for someone as miserable as me." Or do you think, "Praise God! If He says that I should have that, then nothing can stop His blessing from manifesting in my life!"

Unfortunately, too many pick the first one. Just like the Israelites standing on the bank of the Jordan looking at what was promised them, we too often choose to give up before the battle even begins.

Did you know that some of the greatest Christians of all time were lawyers? Now, we tend to make fun of lawyers and politicians in our culture today, but throughout history, lawyers have revealed some of the greatest things about God we have ever known. Moses was "the lawgiver," and the apostle Paul was a Pharisee. (The Pharisees were a group who studied the Word of God as the law book on which to govern society.) Martin Luther of the Reformation began his career by entering law school, as did the great revivalist Charles Finney. What made them so powerful? They read their Bibles as lawyers would when studying to prepare a case, and they put more faith in God keeping His Word than they did in any earthly laws or political promises. Then they took those words and charged the atmosphere around them with biblical truth.

Come into agreement with what God has already said in His Word about you and your situation. You have to get God's Word on it. Then fill your atmosphere with His promises on the matter.

Words have power, presence, and prophetic implications. Look what happened when Ezekiel took God at His Word and spoke it into a dead atmosphere:

> Again He said to me, "Prophesy to these bones, and say to them, 'O dry bones, hear the word of the LORD! Thus says the Lord GOD to these bones: "Surely I will cause breath to enter into you, and you shall live...."'"
> So I prophesied as I was commanded; and as I prophesied...the bones came together, bone to bone.
> —Ezekiel 37:4–7, NKJV

When you read the Bible, you need to take God's Word personally. Put your trust in the fact that His promises are for His people, and that means YOU. Speak life into your dead areas—you'll be amazed at what God's words in your mouth will do for you.

If God has said it, then that should settle it for us.

Cindy Trimm, *Commanding Your Morning* (Lake Mary, FL: Charisma House, 2007), 59–62.

EIGHT

NOT IF, *but* WHEN

by
Judy Jacobs

Jesus said, "When you pray," not if, or just in case an opportunity would present itself, but very emphatically, "When you pray," as if to say, "This is to be done without even thinking about it." There seems to be an epidemic of prayerlessness that has hit the church in recent years that is numbing.

God told the children of Israel in Numbers 15:1–2, "The Lord told Moses to give these instructions to the people of Israel: '*When* your children finally live in the land I am going to give them...'" (TLB, emphasis added). Not if, but when. The children of Israel couldn't see the promises of God. They couldn't see themselves in the Promised Land flowing with milk and honey. All they could see were the giants, enemies on every hand, the cloud by day, the fire by night, all that manna. But God had emphatically given them a time frame—a "when." In other words, "I know what it looks like and what it might seem like, but I have spoken and I cannot go back on My word." God is bound by His word, which is the reason why we must remind God of what He said.

If God said "when" back then, He is still saying "when" today. Everything that God has said shall—and will—come to pass.

Paul said, "Being confident [fully persuaded] of this very thing, that he which hath begun a good work in you will perform [finish] it until the day of Jesus Christ" (Phil. 1:6). You pay your tithe because you are fully persuaded that "God shall supply all your need according to His riches in glory by Christ Jesus" (Phil. 4:19, NKJV). Fully persuaded, fully convinced that God is going to do what God said in His Word that He will do. Fully persuaded that you will possess the land that God said is yours.

God told the children of Israel to go in and possess the land. But when they got there to possess it, there were giants occupying it. Now may I tell you something? There will always be giants to oppose you and intimidate you. But God has given you purpose, destiny, and abundant grace to finish what He started in your life. Through prayer and violent faith you can stand firm in your confession and believe you are who God says you are.

My dear friend Dr. Myles Munroe states in his book *Understanding the Purpose and Power of Prayer*, "Prayer is man giving God the legal right and permission to interfere in earth's affairs."* Yielded and effective prayer is saying to God, "I give You permission to do what You want to do in my life, when You want to do it, how You want to do it, and where You want to do it." One thing is for sure; prayer is not an option to the believer. Jesus said, "When you pray," and in another passage He said, "When you fast," meaning such things are expected.

Jesus said, "Men ought always to pray, and not to faint" (Luke 18:1). In another passage, He says to "pray without ceasing" (1 Thess. 5:17, NKJV). This would suggest a continual

---

* Myles Munroe, *Understanding the Purpose and Power of Prayer* (New Kensington, PA: Whitaker House, 2002).

conversation, a practice that is not unique or something special to be done at certain times or seasons. Jesus plainly instructed us, don't quit praying. "The earnest prayer of a righteous man has great power and wonderful results" (James 5:16, TLB). The key to effective prayer is found in Mark 9:23, "If thou canst believe, all things are possible to him that believeth."

God can shut the mouths of lions, deliver from a fiery furnace, open up the Red Sea, or command the sun and moon to stand still, simply because that's what needs to be done for one of His children.

God doesn't want all of us to quit our jobs, abandon daily life as we know it, and join a monastery to spend the rest of our lives in continuous prayer. But what He does want and expect from us is to stay in communication with Him throughout our day—on purpose—speaking praises, prayers, and petitions and filling our minds with thoughts of Him. Speak things such as, "I love You," "You are my God," "You are the great God," "You are working everything out for my good," "You are with me, so I will not fear," or anything else that comes to mind that you want to say to Him. The Word promises, "Thou wilt keep him in perfect peace, whose mind is stayed on thee: because he trusteth in thee" (Isa. 26:3).

Judy Jacobs, *Take It By Force!* (Lake Mary, FL: Charisma House, 2005), 122–124.

NINE

ARMED WITH HIS MIGHT

by
Judy Jacobs

THE DAYS IN WHICH WE ARE LIVING ARE SOME OF THE MOST exciting in history. But they are not without peril. The kingdom of God suffers violence (Matt. 11:12), yet these are still times of hope and peace for those who know who they are in Christ. In order to survive the onslaught of the enemy against us, we had better learn to become women who are mighty in spirit. During the course of my life, I've found six practices to be very effective in overcoming the power of the enemy and walking in victory.

1. Be confident in your calling

When you are confident in your calling, you don't have to seek anyone's permission or approval. You know you are called because of the witness of the Holy Spirit inside you, but Satan will try to make you doubt that your calling is real.

God never told us that we were going to float along on this journey to become all that He destined for us and never have another problem. But He did promise us this: "When you pass through the waters, I will be with you; and through the rivers, they shall not overflow you" (Isa. 43:2, NKJV). You must decide now that you're going all the way.

2. Have strength in adversity

When I left home to pursue God's call on my life, I knew it was not going to be easy. On the day I was preparing to leave I suddenly thought, "Maybe I should go to church one more time." At the close of the Wednesday night service, my pastor called me onto the stage and said to me: "God says to tell you, 'You are not your own; you have been bought with a price. I have chosen you and appointed you to go to the nations of the earth, so you can't do what you want to do.'"

Without anyone touching me, I was slain in the spirit. Hours later, when I got up, I had a new confidence, a greater boldness, and a determination to go on that hell could not touch.

Jesus said: "You did not choose Me, but I chose you and appointed you that you should go and bear fruit, and that your fruit should remain, that whatever you ask the Father in My name He may give you" (John 15:16, NKJV).

You too are not your own. Be strong and don't abandon your calling.

3. Develop godly character

You must be painstakingly conscientious about everything—attitude, lifestyle, personal worship, and gifts. The enemy of your destiny has already been defeated, so don't allow yourself to be sidetracked by his devices.

4. Practice violent faith

I believe that sometimes we come up against things in our lives when simply believing won't be enough. Violent faith combines determination with spiritual aggressiveness and raw, if you will, guts. As you practice it, your prayer life and hunger for God will increase, and there will be a determination forged in you that nothing can shake.

5. Be persistent in prayer

Taking back what is yours from the forces of darkness takes courage and is not for those who are passive or faint of heart. It is for the person who would say: "This is it. I am drawing the blood line today. I will never be the same again." You can choose to say, "I know what the outcome of this thing is going to be, so I am going to lift my head up and rejoice, because right now the Father God is working it all out."

6. Praise God

One thing I have learned and am still learning is that you don't praise God *when* the answer comes; you praise God *until* the answer comes. Something happens when you lift your hands and your voice to praise God in the midst of all hell surrounding you.

Begin to rejoice in God. See yourself mighty in spirit and walking in victory. What you can see with spirit eyes in the supernatural, you can believe to come forth in the natural.

I see the devil fleeing in terror because you and I are rising up now, and we know that "the weapons of our warfare are not carnal but mighty in God for pulling down [Satan's] strongholds" (2 Cor. 10:4, NKJV). We are women, mighty in spirit, who are strong in the strength of our Lord. And in His power, we are victorious!

Judy Jacobs, "Armed With His Might," *SpiritLed Woman*, August/September 2005, 16–19.

TEN

TOO BUSY NOT *to* PRAY

by
Quin Sherrer
and
Ruthanne Garlock

I F YOU ARE LIKE MOST OF US THESE DAYS, YOU LIVE A VERY active, crowded life. Finding—or taking—the time to pray may be rather low on your priority list.

But prayer is important because it is actually the link between us and God. It's our way of communicating with Him and listening quietly for His response. You could call it the "divine connection."

What exactly is prayer? In a nutshell: simply talking to God as you would talk to your best friend. Acknowledging Him as your Father. Telling Him your deepest feelings. Honestly admitting your mistakes. Asking for His help, guidance, and wisdom for what you face each day, then waiting for His direction. It also involves intercession for others.

Praying every day does not mean that all our problems will

suddenly vanish. But if we stay connected to our heavenly Father, we will begin to see things from His perspective and find His help to manage our lives.

In instructing His disciples, Jesus said, "When you pray, go into your [most] private room" (Matt. 6:6, AMP). This implies that God desires us to shut ourselves in with Him.

Do you have a secret place where you can go to pray? A particular room, a special chair, a private nook or spot where you can meet with God each day? Jesus frequently found such a place of solitude for prayer, often outdoors (Mark 1:35; Luke 6:12). By both word and example He trained His disciples in the importance of prayer.

The classic prayer that we call the Lord's Prayer is perhaps the most memorized portion of Scripture in the entire Bible. But it is much more than simply a prayer to recite by rote. This model from Jesus's teaching shows us the important elements our personal prayers should include if we want to pray with power:

- Acknowledge God as Father and offer worship to Him.

- Pray for His will to be done in the earth (and submit our will to His).

- Present our personal needs to Him.

- Ask forgiveness for our own sins and offer forgiveness to those who have offended us.

- Ask for divine protection from temptation and the evil one.

- Declare God's almighty power and authority.

Quin Sherrer and Ruthanne Garlock, *Lord, I Need to Pray With Power* (Lake Mary, FL: Charisma House, 2007), 2–4.

ELEVEN

PRAYER THAT LISTENS

by

Quin Sherrer

and

Ruthanne Garlock

WAITING IS NOT A FAVORITE THING FOR MOST OF US. Listening is even further down the list. One of the hardest disciplines during prayer is to wait and listen—for God's direction, assurance, or correction.

Prayer involves having a conversation with God. And He places a lot of emphasis on hearing. For example, in the New King James version of the Bible some form of the word *hear* appears 538 times and *listening* some 112 times. So we would be wise to position ourselves expectantly as we pray, believing we will hear from heaven.

God can speak to us anytime, anyplace, in any manner He wishes. It may be through a Scripture passage that seems to leap off the page into our thoughts, or through words from a song, a sermon, or another person's remark. Or we hear His voice as a whisper in our spirit. But anytime we sense that God is speaking, it's a good idea to grab a pen and write down the message. Then we can recall it later when we need clarity or reassurance.

Sometimes He speaks in our solitude, during complete silence. Other times He may commune with us during a stroll on the sidewalk or beach, a walk through the woods, or while riding in a boat, car, train, or airplane. Some people hear Him while enjoying an invigorating shower or a soak in the tub.

Others find direction as they listen to worship music, letting the words penetrate deep into their spirits. God may speak through dreams or visions, and sometimes through prophets. He can speak while you are working, reading, watching TV, or playing with a child.

Just as babies learn to walk, we grow in our listening skills as we mature in our Christian faith. We also become increasingly grateful when we realize that God Himself—the creator of the universe—wants to speak to us, and not just when we cry out during times of trouble. He knows our individual personalities and how best to communicate with each one of us.

Quin Sherrer and Ruthanne Garlock, *Lord, I Need to Pray With Power* (Lake Mary, FL: Charisma House, 2007), 35–36.

TWELVE

YOU CAN TRUST GOD
WITH YOUR DREAMS

by

Judy Jacobs

ON AUGUST 28, 1963, ON THE STEPS OF THE LINCOLN Memorial in Washington DC, Dr. Martin Luther King Jr., in his greatest speech, declared, "I have a dream...that one day this nation will rise up and live out the true meaning of its creed: 'We hold these truths to be self-evident: that all men are created equal.'"*

Just as Dr. King had a dream, I too have a dream.

I have a dream...

- To see my little girls grow up knowing that they are valued, anointed, appointed, and made in the image of God

- To see people fulfill their potential, regardless of race, color, or gender

---

* Martin Luther King Jr., "I Have a Dream," http://www.usconstitution .net/dream.html (accessed June 20, 2007).

- That the people of God will not be bound by traditions hindering them from fulfilling lives and from obeying the call of God on their lives

- To see every sick body healed and to see the body of Christ walking in health, wholeness, and prosperity

- To see revival and reformation come that will bring a sweeping of souls that will be unprecedented

- That the church will catch the jet stream of revival and grab hold of the quickening wind of the Holy Spirit to see the Great Commission come forth

I had dreams of having a ministry to see people saved, set free, and delivered. I had dreams of doing a live recording, writing a book, organizing a women's conference, and hosting a mentoring institute. All of these were dreams—big dreams—but then again, I know that I serve a big God.

To each one of us there has been given a capacity to dream. Jesus called it faith. Paul said, "God hath dealt to every man the measure of faith" (Rom. 12:3). The Bible speaks of many degrees of faith. It says to some He gave great faith, others were full of faith, and He gave to others little faith, and still to others weak faith, but nevertheless, faith. (See Matthew 8; 14; Acts 6; Romans 14.) Faith and dreams go hand in hand.

Maybe you feel as if your dreams have died a long time ago, or maybe you feel your dream is not so much dead, but buried, or maybe even asleep. I want this chapter to be a word from the Lord to quicken those dreams back to life again. Paul said:

> And you *hath he quickened*, who were dead in trespasses and sins....But God, who is rich in mercy, for his great love wherewith he loved us, even when we were dead in sins, hath quickened us together with Christ, (by grace ye are saved;)

and hath raised us up together, and made *us* sit together in *heavenly* places in Christ Jesus.

—Ephesians 2:1, 4–6, emphasis added

The word *quickened* is a very interesting word. In this context, it means, "to revive, to hasten, to show signs of life." It reminds me of the quickening a woman experiences during pregnancy. When I was pregnant with our first child, I can remember the first time I felt that precious little baby move inside me. This movement is known as "quickening." The joy and excitement that I felt was inexpressible. She was letting Jamie and me know, "Yes, I'm alive inside here. I am active. I'm coming in just a few short months. Your dream is going to be born."

It is time for you to experience a quickening in your spirit and realize you need to take action to see those dreams begin to live again. Paul said, "Awake, O sleeper, rise up from the dead, and Christ will give you light" (Eph. 5:14, NLT). It is time to revive those dreams and bring light where there has been darkness. Let me ask you a question: what do you do with something that is dead? Some might say, "You bury it." But I say, no, you don't bury it, but in the name of Jesus, you resurrect it! God is going to give you the strength to call those dreams that are not, done! I believe that everything dead in your life is about to be resurrected.

But for every dream there is a striking reminder that there will be a price to pay to see those dreams birthed. Dr. King paid with his life, and for some of you, there will be a price to pay. It may be your reputation, your status in the community, being known as one of those "faith people," or it may be dying to self—to what you want or desire. Whatever the price, are you willing to go all the way?

Judy Jacobs, *Take It By Force!* (Lake Mary, FL: Charisma House, 2005), 169, 171.

THIRTEEN

GOD WANTS YOU *to* KNOW HIS PURPOSE *for* YOUR LIFE

by

Fuchsia Pickett

MY ENTIRE LIFE WAS CHANGED BY THE DISCOVERY OF this one truth: the destiny of my life is hinged upon understanding God's eternal purpose, which He unveiled to man through His sacrificial love.

I was not aware of this powerful truth, despite the fact that I had finished my graduate studies in theology, including rewriting the five hundred cardinal doctrines of the church for my thesis. Through my studies I had learned how to investigate the great truths of the Bible and thought I knew something about almost every doctrine. I prided myself on my attempts to be an exegetical theologian, pastoring and carefully teaching the Word in Bible colleges for seventeen years.

However, it wasn't until after I received the baptism of the Holy Spirit, which brought me into a greater relationship with the divine teacher, that I discovered the great truth of the critical importance of understanding God's eternal purpose.

Truth has the incredible power to free man of despair, hopelessness, and a meaningless existence, and to create in him a sense of destiny and purpose that can motivate him to greatness. Jesus said of Himself, "I am...the truth" (John 14:6). To believe in Jesus involves receiving the truth of His teachings and allowing them to change your thinking, your values, and your behavior. The words of the devil—the lies that are working in your life to destroy you—are only exposed as they are contrasted with truth. In the light of truth, those lies lose their seductive power, and you are set free from their destruction.

Freedom is the scriptural promise to all who walk in truth. "Ye shall know the truth, and the truth shall make you free" (John 8:32). That promise gives each of us hope to become the person God intended us to be as we walk in His truth. If you want to know real meaning and purpose in your life, your home, and your church, it is necessary that you pursue God's truth.

God's eternal purpose will be realized in your individual life, in your home, and ultimately in the church as you are conformed to the image of Christ through the working of the Holy Spirit in you. If you are to fully understand God's purpose for you, you will need to cultivate a relationship with the Holy Spirit. Learn to understand who He is. Cooperate with Him as He works to fulfill God's purpose for mankind.

Fuchsia Pickett, *God's Purpose for You* (Lake Mary, FL: Charisma House, 2003), 4–5, 21.

SECTION TWO

BECOMING *a* WOMAN *of* LOVE

FOURTEEN

BECAUSE *of* GOD, MY PAST IS NOT MY FUTURE

by

Lisa Bevere

ARE YOU IN CHRIST? THEN YOU MUST LET GO OF THE old. It is gone, and a new way of living has been prepared for you. You must use your gift of faith to step into this new life. Let go of your past, because your past is not your future.

God is the Lord of our future. He has plans for us. He is always planning ahead so we don't have to. All we have to do is trust Him and learn His ways. His ways are higher and wiser, and He clearly tells us to forget our past.

Philippians 3:13–14 instructs us to forget what is behind. It exhorts us to strain for what is ahead, loosing ourselves of the load of our past. That is the only way we can have the necessary strength to persevere to our goal.

How many marathon runners carry backpacks? If they started with one, it would soon be dropped in order to lighten their load so they could finish their race. Marathon runners compete in the lightest apparel possible and carry only what is necessary for their journey.

We also run a race. It is not only a physical race but also a spiritual one. That is what makes this race different.

Proverbs 4:18 tells us that the path becomes clearer and more distinct as we walk it: "The path of the righteous is like the first gleam of dawn, shining ever brighter till the full light of day" (NIV). As long as we go forward, our light will increase. We can't go forward when we are looking back, so we must turn to the Son and follow His light. With each step, we leave the realm of darkness and travel deeper into His light, until it shines brighter than the full light of day.

Some of you are running with backpacks filled with stones because you are trying to bring your past into the future. Others of you are looking back. Maybe you are afraid your future will be like your past. Now is the time to put the past to rest.

When we excuse our behavior by our past, we say, "I've earned the right to be this way because of what was done to me." This attitude betrays the presence of unforgiveness in our hearts. Forgiveness is the very foundation of the gospel. Without forgiveness, there is no remission of sin. Unforgiveness will keep us bound to our past.

> Do not judge, and you will not be judged. Do not condemn, and you will not be condemned. Forgive, and you will be forgiven.
>
> —Luke 6:37, NIV

Unforgiveness inevitably causes us to lose sight of our own need of forgiveness. We have God's promise that if we forgive, we will be forgiven. It is when we don't forgive that the weight of our own sins comes back to bear down on us. The forgiveness of God is the very force that releases us from our past. We can even release others, for "if you forgive anyone his sins, they are forgiven; if you do not forgive them, they are not forgiven" (John 20:23, NIV). But remember—by not forgiving others, we are also not forgiven. Some of us have withheld forgiveness as a form of punishment...when in the end we are only punishing ourselves. Is it worth it?

Lisa Bevere, *The True Measure of a Woman* (Lake Mary, FL: Charisma House, 1997, 2007), 76–78.

FIFTEEN

GETTING EVERYTHING OUT *of* LIFE

by

Cindy Trimm

Have you ever had the gnawing feeling on the inside that you were not getting everything you were supposed to get out of life? A feeling that life was full of possibilities, but somehow you could never figure out how to tap into them? Have you ever looked at another person's life, marriage, financial status, or career and wondered, "What's wrong with me?" Well, you are not alone.

Many people have come to believe that life is a mystery that cannot be solved. They think that success and prosperity are destined for everyone except them, and they feel powerless and victimized as the events of their lives spiral out of control. They would do something about it if they knew what to do, but the truth of the matter is, they have tried everything they know and come up empty every time. What they need is a new set of keys to unlock all that God is holding for them in their lives, keys that will help you escape these "prisons of the mind."

Still, there are others who may experience short seasons of success, but then despairingly long seasons of trials, tribulation, setbacks, and lack. Their lives are governed by success-undermining phrases such as: "Stuff happens," "Life is unpredictable," "All good things must come to an end," "If it is not one thing, it's another," and "This is as good as it gets." These folks are ignorant of the fact that they are victims of their own self-fulfilling prophecies.

We need to realize that the Word of God has the power to realign anything that is misaligned, especially faulty mindsets, belief systems, ideologies, traditions, and doctrines of deception that lie and exalt themselves above the will of God for your life. Life does not have to be a mystery for you. You do not have to continue mindlessly groping in the dark for the right path through life. God already has your success, prosperity, and fulfillment all planned out; you just have to follow His directions to find it. As the Scriptures say:

> For I know the thoughts that I think toward you, says the LORD, thoughts of peace and not of evil, to give you a future and a hope.
>
> —Jeremiah 29:11, NKJV

You can take control of your life and experience divine success and prosperity by following God's directions outlined in His Word. He has a wonderful plan for you—and His plan for your personal world depends on you fulfilling it by first taking control of your mind and your mouth. Learn to fill your thoughts and words with light and truth.

Cindy Trimm, *Commanding Your Morning* (Lake Mary, FL: Charisma House, 2007), xvii–xix.

SIXTEEN

MASTERING MY THOUGHTS

by
Cindy Trimm

THE POWER OF THE SPOKEN WORD IS ONE OF LIFE'S greatest mysteries. All that you will ever be or accomplish hinges on how you choose to govern what comes out of your mouth. You can either bless your life to great heights of success or send it orbiting into realms of failure, sadness, and discontentment by what you allow to occupy your mind and mouth. This is why Proverbs tells us, "For as he thinks in his heart, so is he" (Prov. 23:7, AMP), and urges, "Guard your heart above all else, for it determines the course of your life" (Prov. 4:23, NLT). Jesus followed suit by declaring, "For whatever is in your heart determines what you say. A good person produces good things from the treasury of a good heart, and an evil person produces evil things from the treasury of an evil heart" (Matt. 12:34–35, NLT).

Just as what occupies your mind determines what eventually fills your mouth, your outer world showcases all that has dominated—and at times subjugated—your inner world.

Because the law of cause and effect is continually at work, there is always an inner cause for every outer effect. In other words, your outer world is a direct result of your inner world. Every circumstance in life is a result of a choice—and every choice is the result of a thought. All those things that fill your mind hold the keys to your reality. Your thoughts provide the fuel for your words, and your words provide the fuel for your world.

Hosea, the prophetic sage of old, said, "For they sow the wind, and they shall reap the whirlwind" (Hos. 8:7, ESV). In other words, each one of us must take responsibility for what we experience in life. We are the sum total of every choice that we have ever made or let happen without our intervention. If you do not like where you are, you are only one thought away from turning toward the life you desire.

If this is to happen, though, it is paramount that you become the master of your thoughts. Sift your thought life. Filter out anything that you do not want to show up in your future and focus on what you truly desire. God wired your thoughts to have power so you would be equipped to overcome every obstacle. He fashioned you to create, innovate, strategize, and succeed—and just to be sure, He put His own divine thoughts and nature within you. As God says in Jeremiah 31:33 (NLT):

> I will put my instructions deep within them, and I will write them on their hearts.

Hook up your heart with the ultimate power source.

Cindy Trimm, *Commanding Your Morning* (Lake Mary, FL: Charisma House, 2007), 4–6.

SEVENTEEN

I'M NEVER ALONE BECAUSE
GOD IS WITH ME

by

Joyce L. Rodgers

IT IS POSSIBLE TO BE ALONE AND FEEL COMPLETELY HAPPY and satisfied in one's heart. But it is also possible to be lonely in a crowd. To be alone is to be "separated from others: isolated, exclusive of anyone or anything else." *Loneliness* is defined as "the state of being lonely, being without company, desolate, producing a feeling of bleakness or desolation." Loneliness can cause you to lose sight of the promise made by Jesus: "I will never leave thee, nor forsake thee" (Heb. 13:5).

Loneliness is largely dependent upon where you are mentally, not physically. A woman can be married, have a house full of children, or be surrounded by co-workers and friends, and yet she could be the loneliest person around. Her sense of isolation is usually internal, and she may believe that if she were to articulate her feelings to anyone, she would be met with derision or even rebuke. "How can you be lonely," people would ask, "when you have such a wonderful husband and two beautiful children?" Despite the people around her, the reality of loneliness covers her like a shroud.

Sometimes people are lonely but don't even realize it. We can cover up our loneliness in so many ways: by throwing ourselves into the hustle and bustle of life, filling our houses with material possessions, or even busying ourselves with church work rather than kingdom work. If we do not address the root of our loneliness, it will gnaw at our hearts.

Thank God we have a High Priest who can sympathize with our loneliness. All of Jesus's disciples and friends abandoned Him in the hours before He faced the cross. Jesus said: "The hour cometh, yea, is now come, that ye shall be scattered, every man to his own, and shall leave me alone: and yet I am not alone, because the Father is with me" (John 16:32).

Jesus's words in this passage are so simple yet so profound. In them lies our answer to loneliness: we are never alone, and there is no need to feel lonely, because God is with us!

Lonely heart, allow the loving hand of God to reach down into your mind, heart, and spirit and drive out the feelings of isolation and disconnection that plague you. Realize that a true sense of connection and completeness will never come from factors outside you; it can only come from within you. Stop seeking fulfillment and identity from external sources, especially from other people, for disappointment often causes retreat—and isolation and loneliness will soon follow. Denounce loneliness and seize the day! Embrace the will and plan of God for your life, and let your wholeness come from Him in whom there is no lack, only inexhaustible supply.

Joyce L. Rodgers, *Fatal Distractions* (Lake Mary, FL: Charisma House, 2003), 114–117.

EIGHTEEN

WHAT'S WRONG WITH MY ATTITUDE?

by

Cathy Lechner

Have you ever heard the famous saying, "Your attitude determines your altitude"?

I once read a story about a group of people who were determined to climb a particular mountain. No one had ever succeeded because the conditions were beyond human capability of withstanding.

The higher they went, the slower they climbed. As the journey progressed, one by one, men began to drop out and, with sadness, turn back.

They had spent years planning, raising money, and making precious preparations as they lived, slept, and talked about the climb. They were consumed by their dream. Although they knew that they were risking their lives to reach the top of the mountain, it was worth it all to them.

Now, even though they thought they had planned for every conceivable problem, the unpredictability of the journey caught them off guard. Several of them turned back, bitterly disappointed. Two died. Another lost fingers, toes, and his nose due to severe frostbite, barely escaping with his life.

Finally, only two of the men gasped for oxygen and huddled in a tent on the side of the mountain. Caught in an unexpected blinding ice and snow storm, they took videos of each other. They wanted to capture what they thought would be their last words as a legacy to their families.

Miraculously, those two lived. They brought back hard-won knowledge and wisdom and once again began to assemble another team to climb the mountain.

I honestly don't get it. Of course, just standing on the top of a three-step stool makes me dizzy and nauseous. In order to entice me up a mountain, you would have to promise me that I would receive an angelic visitation and that a box of money and several pounds of fudge were waiting at the top.

Just like those climbers, we can plan and prepare and do everything right. However, life is filled with things that we never learned about in Sunday school, Bible school, or "Training for Reigning" class.

The majority will not make it, simply because it is not easy. Much of our success depends on fortitude, but most of our ability to survive is rooted in attitude.

Just a pebble in their boot is enough to make some turn back. Suffering does not create your spirit. Suffering only reveals your spirit.

Cathy Lechner, *You've Got to Be Kidding, I Thought This Was the Great Tribulation!* (Lake Mary, FL: Charisma House, 1999), 22–23.

NINETEEN

The POWER *of* PROACTIVE PERMISSION

by

Cindy Trimm

WHEN GOD MADE THE DECLARATION "LET THERE BE light," He was really saying, "I allow light to be." He was giving the light, straining at its harnesses to exist in the spirit, permission to manifest itself in the physical world. We must understand there are prohibiting, spiritual forces at work able to keep these things from occurring. There are fallen angels that cause deviations to what God originally purposed working in opposition to what God wants for your life—they operate much like the heavenly angels assigned to bring about the manifestation to your prayers, only in the exact opposite way. According to Scripture, demonic forces were once angels who had been given the same original assignment of responding to voice-activated commands, but when they fell from heaven, their mission became perverted—so instead of bringing the answers, they prohibit answers from manifesting. Your faith attracts the attention of heaven's angels to work on your behalf, while your fear draws the demons of hell to work against you. Your words become the magnet that draws either heaven or hell into your situation.

Always remember, no force is more powerful than the spoken word of God. The Bible says the power of life and death is in your tongue. (See Proverbs 18:21.) It is the Word of God that comes forth from your mouth that pulls all the resources of heaven into your situation. (See Matthew 18:18.) In her book *Live a Praying Life*, Jennifer Kennedy Dean writes, "In response to our prayers, spiritual forces are set in motion that bring God's will to earth. Prayer has its first effect in the spiritual realm. When the work is finished in the spiritual realm, the answer is revealed in the material realm."*

John Wesley once said, "It seems God is limited by our prayer life—that He can do nothing for humanity unless someone asks Him."** Throughout the Bible we learn that God cannot intervene on the earth unless someone gives permission for the answer to exist in the material world. Answers are held up in the heavens and locked up in the realm of the spirit until there is a person able to pick up on the correct frequency and act as a conduit to release God's will into the earth.

This is illustrated by Jacob's experience in the Book of Genesis. God gave Jacob a vision of a ladder going up to heaven—the top of the ladder touched heaven and the bottom touched the earth. There were angels ascending and descending—much like radio waves would move along an antennae. This is exactly how divine inspiration works. Here God was speaking to Jacob's mind and enabling him to pick up

---

* Jennifer Kennedy, *Live a Praying Life* (Birmingham, AL: New Hope Publishers, 2006), 59.
** As quoted in Germaine Copeland, "Too Busy to Pray," Prayers.org, March 2003, http://www.prayers.org/articles/article_mar03.asp (accessed June 7, 2007).

a spiritual frequency. When he got tuned into this frequency, he saw how the invisible realm was manifesting itself in the visible realm.

Sometimes our thoughts are like these frequencies. Jacob saw a ladder, and that was the modern technology of his day. But in the twenty-first century he might have seen a wireless computer or cell phone. Jacob was able to get a glimpse of a spiritual superhighway. I believe these superhighways are our thoughts—this is where we pick up inspiration—these inspirational thoughts seem to appear out of thin air, but really they are circulating in the realm of the spirit.

God gave Moses a divine inspiration—a vision of the heavenly tabernacle. He gave Moses a vision of something that already existed in heaven—the actual spiritual tabernacle. God opened up the eyes of Moses and he was able to see it and replicate it here in the earth. Secret things belong unto God, but those things which are revealed belong unto man. (See Deuteronomy 29:29.) It is a point of revelation—a point of inspiration—where God wants to speak to us all. He said "I know the thoughts that I think toward you...thoughts of peace, and not of evil, to give you an expected end" (Jer. 29:11). He knows the end from the beginning and He knows everything in between—and those are the things that He wants to reveal to you.

Cindy Trimm, *Commanding Your Morning* (Lake Mary, FL: Charisma House, 2007), 71–74.

TWENTY

IS ANGER TAKING OVER MY LIFE?

by

Joyce L. Rodgers

SOLOMON, THE WISEST MAN—ASIDE FROM CHRIST—TO EVER live on the earth, had these words to say about a woman who was continually angry: "It is better to dwell in the wilderness, than with a contentious and an angry woman" (Prov. 21:19). Remember, this advice was coming from a man who himself had seven hundred wives and three hundred concubines (1 Kings 11:3). Solomon knew what he was talking about!

In addition to the anger that arises from dissatisfaction with one's self, fatal anger can arise within a woman who is angry with herself. A woman who is angry with herself has not forgiven herself. Think about it: a woman who has not forgiven herself for her own illegitimate pregnancy will usually be especially harsh toward or critical of unwed teenage mothers. If a woman is overweight and has not "forgiven" herself for her physical appearance, she will be defensive and easily offended by women who are "skinny." A person who has "forgiven much, loves much," and when we are able to forgive ourselves for our own indiscretions and shortcomings, we are not as easily tempted to strike out against others.

Just as not forgiving ourselves will cause us to be angry women, harboring unforgiveness toward others will also cause us to lash out in anger. In addition to the sin of expressing hostile anger toward someone, if we refuse forgiveness to her, we cut off the flow of forgiveness that God would extend toward us. "For if ye forgive men their trespasses," Jesus said, "your heavenly Father will also forgive you: But if you forgive not men their trespasses, neither will your Father forgive your trespasses" (Matt. 6:14–15).

Forgiveness can loosen the hold of unresolved anger, anger than has not yet been dealt with successfully. It takes the grace of God to let go of anger and release forgiveness in heartbreaking situations, but it is possible, for we can "do everything through him [Christ] who gives [us] strength" (Phil. 4:13, NIV).

Indulging your anger makes you reactive instead of proactive. Rather than addressing a situation and anticipating future problems before it gets out of control, you explosively respond to whatever is confronting you. Being prone to excessive anger shows that you have problems in your own life. I urge you to identify quickly those broken areas and then ask God to help you rebuild those areas before the enemy tries to ensnare you even further.

Shore yourself up in repentance and prayer, and ask God to reveal to you exactly what it is that is making you angry. If you must be angry at something, be angry at the way anger is destroying your life and the lives of those you love!

Joyce L. Rodgers, *Fatal Distractions* (Lake Mary, FL: Charisma House, 2003), 121, 124–126.

TWENTY-ONE

OVERCOMING *the* TRAP *of* *an* UNHEALTHY LIFESTYLE

by

Pamela M. Smith

LIVING LIFE IN THE TWENTY-FIRST CENTURY MEANS living tough lives—financially, relationally, politically, emotionally, and spiritually. I see the world running on two unhealthy tracks for survival in these tough times. One is a chronic lack of self-care manifested in unhealthy eating, high stress levels, and near-empty energy supplies. The other is an obsessive-compulsive drive for beautiful, superhuman bodies—and the belief that if our bodies are perfect, our lives will be perfect. Often we find ourselves bouncing like a pinball between the two.

We have been designed and destined for a lifestyle of freedom. Yet, no matter what popular thought may say, we are not born free; we are born to be free. Spiritual freedom comes with knowing God and His desires for our lives.

It breaks His heart when He sees us ensnared in the traps of the world. He knows that if we are caught in struggles over food, we are not free to work on our heart issues. We are not free to love God—and others—as we love ourselves.

As you embark on your journey to freedom and wellness, you must renew your commitment each day to living free. Take a daily diversion. My life, like yours, is so full of demands that I must have regular, replenishing investments from God. I require quietness to hear the gentle voice of God, to seek His ways and ask His guidance. In the quiet times, He comforts and encourages me.

Information does not change lives; revelation does. Grasp hold of one truth and let it take root in you and change your life. Each day, every moment of the day, we have voices within casting a vote over us. The enemy of life casts a vote of hopelessness and unworthiness. That voice says, "You can never change. Look at the life you've had, what you've done, what's been done to you." The enemy has come to steal our hope—to rob us of our self-worth and keep us feeling useless.

But there is also a vote cast over us that is a vote of truth: We are mighty overcomers who have been given a hope and a future.

Each one of us has the deciding vote. We break the tie. With whom will we side? Let us vote for truth!

To succeed in any lifestyle change, we must draw upon God's power. He wants to renew our minds and show us His perspective. He works progressively over time. As we wait for Him to work, He gives us power to transform. His desire is for us to "prosper in all things and be in health" (3 John 2, NKJV).

Pamela M. Smith, *Food for Life* (Lake Mary, FL: Siloam, 1994, 1997, 2004), 18, 209–210.

TWENTY-TWO

SPRING-CLEANING *for* YOUR FINANCES

by

Catherine Eagan

GOD HAS A POWERFUL WAY OF ANNOUNCING THE CHANGE of season from winter to spring. The scent of lilacs fills the air. Warm breezes invite us to throw open our windows. Parks turn pink with blooming azaleas. Tulips and daffodils push their heads out of the unthawed ground.

Spring is the time of year that women traditionally think about giving their houses a thorough cleaning and making everything fresh and new. The types of spring-cleaning we can embark upon in our day are nearly endless: cleaning computer hard drives, emptying e-mail boxes, and uncluttering everything and anything in summer homes, parents' homes, and garages.

However, I seldom hear anyone talk about spring cleaning her finances. Few conversations focus on taking inventory of bank accounts; looking over credit card statements and credit reports; assessing investments, including IRA, 401(k), and

403(b) accounts; or reviewing wills, estate plans, beneficiaries, and insurance limits and deductions.

We rarely spend a season of time and energy refreshing assets that are depreciating or marginally appreciating. Some of us would do well this spring to leave the cobwebs in the house up a little while longer and allow the Holy Spirit to help us get a fresh new start financially.

Spring-cleaning your finances is mandatory if you want God to move. As women, we have so many household responsibilities that we can become overwhelmed trying to single-handedly serve God; help our husbands, kids, and parents, whether young or old; manage homes; and still have the clarity of mind to organize our money.

But spring-cleaning your finances isn't difficult. Here's how to do it in six days.

Day 1: Take inventory of your assets and liabilities. This involves four steps: (1) completing a financial statement; (2) reviewing all assets and confirming current values; (3) listing all liabilities, including debts, obligations, loans, and notes; and (4) determining your net worth.

Day 2: Review monthly statements and expenses. This includes bank statements, credit card statements, investment reports, and recurring bills such as those for utilities and telephone service. On itemized statements, look for any accounting errors or inappropriate fee charges. Review your credit card interest rates. They are negotiable, particularly if you have a timely payment history in the last twelve months.

Day 3: Analyze annual documents. These include your social security statements; home, condo, and apartment insurance policies; health and disability insurance coverage; life insurance policies; credit report; and tax returns. Credit scores are as valuable as money. The median FICO score is 723. Anything less will cost you money in interest rates, mortgages, car loans, insurance policies, loans, business opportunities, and today even employment. If you have an excellent score, maintain it aggressively, check your credit report annually, and guard against identity theft, a rapidly growing crime.

Day 4: Review investment strategies for retirement planning. Consider IRA and Roth IRA contributions, 401(k) and 403(b) contributions, annuities, individually held stocks and bonds, and mutual funds. Undertake a wholesale evaluation of your investment portfolio, and if you don't have one, begin putting money aside today. Review for proper diversification and asset reallocation to achieve higher total returns. If you can, contribute the maximum in any company-matched, tax-deferred contribution plans; this is free money in your pocket.

Day 5: Estate planning review (every three years). Determine ownership or incidence of ownership for everything in your estate. Also take the following steps:

- Review your will.
- Review beneficiaries.
- Determine patient advocacy.
- Designate guardians and custodians.
- Reexamine trust agreements.

Day 6: Evaluate your financial advisers. These would include personal financial planners, legal counselors, stockbrokers or money managers, loan and mortgage bankers, coaches and mentors, and insurance agents.

Jesus once told a story about a woman who had ten silver coins and loses one. Then He asked His listeners: "Does she not light a lamp, sweep the house and search carefully until she finds it? And when she finds it, she calls her friends and neighbors together and says, 'Rejoice with me; I have found my lost coin'" (Luke 15:8–9, NIV).

Women of God, it's time for you to start searching for the "lost coins" in your budget that you can use to improve your financial situation. Happy spring-cleaning!

Catherine Eagan, "Spring Cleaning for Your Finances," *SpiritLed Woman*, April/May 2007, 34–38.

TWENTY-THREE

TEACH ME *to* BE *a* SERVANT LIKE CHRIST

by

Babbie Mason

Dr. Paul L. Walker, general international over-seer for the Church of God, Cleveland, Tennessee, once spoke these eloquent words at the funeral of my dear friend's mother. "Man has learned to transmit his voice across paper-thin wire to communicate with someone else on the other side of the globe. Man has learned to use a scalpel to operate between the beats of a heart. But one great lesson man has failed to learn is the lesson on how to be a servant. If you aim to be a great leader, you will always be disappointed. People don't want to be led. But if you desire to be a great servant, you will never be disappointed."

Jesus, the Master Servant, taught His disciples a great lesson on service in Mark 9:35: "If anyone desires to be first, he must be last of all, and servant of all" (AMP). In God's economy, the one who is the least is the one who is the greatest. Jesus, from His very first breath as a baby in a barnyard manger to His very last breath as the Savior at Calvary, exhibited the life of a servant.

Genuine servants are those who know it's not necessary to have great talent or financial resources in order to be used. They just show up, in obedience, with whatever is in their hand. The widow from Zarephath in 1 Kings 17 had a handful of flour in the jar and a little oil in the bottle when the prophet Elijah arrived on her doorstep and asked her to prepare him a meal. Verse 15 says she did what she was asked to do, and she, the prophet Elijah, and her son ate for many days. God delights in and rewards those who bring their gifts to Him in faith and obedience.

It's just like God to use the simplest thing to confound man's sophisticated ways of reasoning and rationalizing. In the Gospel of John, Jesus uses a little boy's lunch of two small fish and five small loaves of bread to feed a multitude of five thousand very hungry people (John 6:9–13). It's not about the gift; it's about what the Giver can do with it. Whether sitting in a house in Zarephath, distributing five thousand fish sandwiches to a very hungry multitude on a hillside, or teaching children in a Sunday school class, little is much when God is in it.

Great singers and great orators are easy to find. People with talent are everywhere. But a great servant is a rare and precious jewel. Real servants teach us more by what they do than by what they say. They give of what is in their hearts as well as what is in their hands. Without servants to warm us with their gracious deeds that often go unappreciated, the world would be a much colder place. Horace Traubel said it best, "If the world is cold, make it your business to build fires."

Babbie Mason, *Treasures of Heaven in the Stuff of Earth* (Lake Mary, FL: Charisma House, 2000), 23, 26–27.

TWENTY-FOUR

I'M LEARNING *to* TRANSFER CONTROL *to* GOD

by

Lisa Bevere

Malachi 4:2 (NIV) tells us:

> But for you who revere my name, the sun of righteousness will rise with healing in its wings. And you will go out and leap like calves released from the stall.

Have you ever seen a calf released from its stall? As soon as the door is opened it bolts, leaping, kicking, bounding, and stretching. Watching this, you begin to wonder how the stall ever contained it!

God used this analogy to describe the release of His own people, those who revere and honor His name. They had been pinned up in a stall. Now He wants them free to feed and frolic in the fields.

Notice that before He frees them He is going to heal them. His sun of righteousness will arise with healing. The sun is a ball of constant and consuming fire. We can be certain God is speaking about fire, for in Malachi 4:1 (NIV) it says:

> "Surely the day is coming; it will burn like a furnace. All the arrogant and every evildoer will be stubble, and that day that is coming will set them on fire," says the LORD Almighty. "Not a root or a branch will be left to them."

This describes the refining fire of God's judgment on the proud and wicked. It will burn them until there is nothing left. The same fire that destroys them will purify and heal the believers who love and fear God. The Word of God gives light and life to us, but the same Word pronounces judgment on the world of unbelievers.

After God heals and releases us, we will "trample down the wicked; they will be ashes under the soles of your feet on the day when I do these things" (Mal. 4:3, NIV). Are you ready to be released?

I have shared candidly in the hope that through my openness you might glimpse yourself. It is my prayer that by freely sharing my bondage you can identify with Christ's process of liberation. I have written this from my heart to yours.

Something higher awaits you, a freedom like none you've ever known. It is a priceless freedom that you must fight to maintain. Yet you must allow God to be the One to judge those around you. You need only to submit to God's refining and healing process.

I believe the truths in this book are part of that process. You will know the truth, and it will set you free. It will release you from all captivity.

Now it is time to trample and tread underfoot every yoke of bondage and weight that the enemy has laid upon your shoulders. Throw off the yoke of control. Give God the care of everything. Release it all.

I want you to envision any care or hindrance that weighs you down as the yoke of bondage. Lift it off your shoulders, and throw it at your feet. Write down your cares on a sheet of paper, and place it on the floor. Now address it in prayer:

> *Control and fear, I address you in the name of Jesus. I refuse to be under your bondage or servitude. I renounce your burden. I will take no yoke of religion or fear of man. I am only yoked alongside my Master, Jesus Christ. I relinquish control of my life, family, friends, finances, security, and position. I trample you under my feet to signify that the fire of God has broken your hold from my life.*

Thanks be to God who gives us the victory!

Lisa Bevere, *Out of Control and Loving It!* (Lake Mary, FL: Charisma House, 1996, 2006), 181–182.

TWENTY-FIVE

BEAUTY FROM *the* INSIDE OUT

by
Janet Maccaro

Beauty truly does radiate from within. A healthy, vibrant woman defies age. As a testimony and reflection of our self-esteem, inner beauty, and vibrancy, true beauty is the result of inner vitality, balance, health, and happiness, not vanity.

Optimal nutrition, stress-relieving exercise, and a positive frame of mind are requirements you must tote along on your continued journey toward complete balance. A balanced body and a beautiful spirit are better than the very best cosmetic application or surgery.

With proper nutrition, rest, relaxation, and exercise, you can keep your body balanced, healthy, and youthful throughout your entire life. Your skin can be wrinkle free and elastic, your eyes can sparkle, your complexion can be smooth, and your face can be firm and tight.

When it comes to aging, there are two choices: you either embrace it, or you try to erase it with cosmetic procedures.

However, you can begin feeling and looking better—and younger—if you're willing to make simple lifestyle changes and adjust your health and beauty regimen.

When we are young, our skin is soft, supple, and glowing. Beautiful skin comes naturally in our youth. But, as we age, beautiful skin is a reward for taking proper care of our bodies. The skin is a barometer that reflects what is going on with us internally. Skin care is big business these days as baby boomers anxiously take part in staving off the signs of aging.

Stress, excessive sun exposure, liver malfunction, hormone depletion, smoking, alcohol, sugar, fried foods, caffeine, and poor circulation all contribute to the condition of our skin. Age spots, wrinkles, dry skin, uneven skin tone, sallow complexion, and acne are the result of how well our systems handle wastes.

For healthy, glowing skin, the following simple practices will greatly benefit you:

Skin Care Therapy

- Drink eight to ten glasses of water each day.

- Add fresh lemon for added benefit.

- Make a fresh "liver cocktail" each day (use a juicer). The juice consists of 2 ounces of beet juice, 3 ounces of carrot juice, and 3 ounces of cucumber juice.

- Avoid sugars, caffeine, and red meat to prevent dehydration.

- Eat fresh fruits and vegetables each day; fruits are wonderful cleaners.

Body Therapy

- Reduce or prevent wrinkles by rubbing papaya skins on the face. (Papain is an enzyme that exfoliates the skin.)

- Manage stress.

- Practice deep breathing.

- Have a massage with almond oil, sesame oil, or wheat germ oil to soften the skin.

- Moisturize immediately after bathing.

- Rub lemon juice on age spots or use 2 percent hydroquinone topical cream to reduce and fade age spots.

- Limit sun exposure and always use a sunblock SPF 15 or more to prevent further damage and to prevent age spots from darkening.

True beauty comes from the inner woman—her essence, her spirit. The Bible tells us: "Do not let your adornment be merely outward—arranging the hair, wearing gold, or putting on fine apparel—rather let it be the hidden person of the heart, with the incorruptible beauty of a gentle and quiet spirit, which is very precious in the sight of God" (1 Pet. 3:3–4, NKJV).

Live a beautiful life—let beauty radiate from your body, mind, and spirit. Physical beauty is only skin deep and fades with the passing of time. But true beauty comes from your core and leaves a lasting impression.

Janet Maccaro, "Beauty From the Inside Out," *SpiritLed Woman,* October/ November 2006, 36–38.

TWENTY-SIX

I'M *a* WOMAN DEFINED *by* GOD

by

Lisa Bevere

WHO DEFINES A WOMAN? WE ALREADY KNOW WE CANNOT trust the definition of our culture, since it defines women in terms of the physical. The goal of a fallen culture is to be sexually attractive because it is emblazoned with lust. (See Romans 1:26–27, NIV.)

Though it begins with apparent innocence, young girls become enmeshed in the fantasy of growing up to be beautiful and desirable. After all, nearly every childhood movie alleges that it is the young and beautiful who marry and find happiness. Yet we've grown up and discovered that attractiveness is not enough to hold a family together. This dream rings hollow in our culture, with more than half of all marriages ending in divorce.

Yet from the very beginning God created women to support, to complete—not to compete. This is the case whether a woman is married or single. Women are nurturers by nature, and this strength can be translated to the professional as well as personal. Whether a woman is a single doctor or a stay-at-home mother, she can still bring the nature of a servant to any level. Not simply because she is a woman but because she is a Christian. We have a genderless command to "above all, love each other deeply, because love covers over a multitude of sins.... Each one should use whatever gift he has receive to serve others, faithfully administering God's grace in its various forms" (1 Pet. 4:8, 10, NIV).

Independent of our marital, professional, or social status, our talents and abilities are not to be used to serve our selves, but to serve others. We each have an opportunity to serve God in our unique sphere of influence. God plants each of us in various soils to accomplish His purpose.

In Christ is embodied every dream and hope, not only in heaven but also as an inheritance for us on Earth. He gives us purpose, plans, and a future. His death defines our life. "When Christ, who is your life, appears, then you also will appear with him in glory" (Colossians 3:4, NIV).

He is our life. Because our lives are hidden in Him, our mind, desires, and affections should be set on things above, not on earthly things. By losing sight of the seen we gain the unseen. At the revelation of God's glory we will be seen for what we really are.

God defines us because He has chosen us. He separated us from the world to bring us back to Himself. He delivered us out of darkness into the light so that we would declare His praises. We belong to Him, purchased by the priceless blood of His Son. Because Jesus thought you were something worth dying for, you can be truly alive. He exchanged His vibrant, abundant life for your gray and lifeless one.

By whose definition will you live?

Lisa Bevere, *You Are Not What You Weigh* (Lake Mary, FL: Siloam, 1998, 2007), 151–152, 157, 159–160.

TWENTY-SEVEN

MY DESTINY IS FULFILLED
at HIS FEET

by

Fuchsia Pickett

THE POWER OF CHOICE THAT GOD HAS GIVEN TO EVERY person cannot be underestimated. How dramatically our right to choose affects the course of our lives! Naomi's choice to return to Bethlehem-Judah would ultimately result in her personal restoration. Ruth's choice to follow Naomi and serve Naomi's God brought her to a wonderful destiny. Orpah's name means "stiff-necked or skull." The decision Orpah made to stay in Moab reflected the inflexible, unyielding character described by her name and resulted in her death in obscurity—she was never heard of again. Such is the end of stiff-necked people. It is better to have a harnessed heart than a stiff neck.

Ruth's name means "friend." She proved her friendship to Naomi and to God by her willingness to leave all she held dear to follow Naomi and serve her God. This beauty of character is to be revealed throughout the rest of the narrative as Ruth gains a reputation in the whole city of Bethlehem-Judah as a virtuous woman.

Ruth's treatise was a sevenfold declaration that revealed her heart's determination. The key words in Ruth's treatise were "I will." These two words expressed the intent of her heart and formed the basis of her decision. As we observe Orpah's tearful decision not to follow Naomi, we understand that Ruth's choice was not based on emotion or sentiment, but on a decision of her will.

Decision itself is exhilarating and refreshing. Some people never know the joys and delights of walking with God because they do not choose to make decisions in favor of God, His Word, and His ways. Decisive people are seldom the subject of continued despair; they are steadfastly minded. As we decide to follow God's will, our decision will have wonderful results in our lives, as Ruth's did.

The treatise of "I wills" made by Ruth consisted of seven elements:

> Whither thou goest, I will go; and where thou lodgest, I will lodge: thy people shall be my people, and thy God my God. Where thou diest, will I die, and there will I be buried: the LORD do so to me, and more also, if ought but death part thee and me.
>
> —Ruth 1:16–17

This last "I will," though not explicitly expressed, is understood, for Ruth was declaring in essence, "I will seal this treatise with a covenant. The Lord do so to me and more also if ought but death part thee and me."

Ruth's resolve is a classic for all of literature. As an expression of love and loyalty, these words cannot be surpassed. Here is supreme devotion; here is love to the uttermost, not only passionately expressed, but as history declares, determinedly fulfilled. The beauty of its form and the utter devotion of a genuine and self-conquering love has made Ruth's vow one that never shall be forgotten. The secret of such love and loyalty is kinship in the matters of the soul and of eternity. There can be no true love, no lasting loyalty, without this kinship of soul and spirit.

Ruth's vow has stamped itself indelibly on the heart of the church. Believers throughout history have followed her example in choosing to live, and die, for God alone. How many have gained their courage to face martyrdom from reading the testimony of Ruth!

Like Ruth, we should resolve to pursue God to the end, casting our lot with the separated, sanctified people of God, cleaving to the eternal God of the Bible. Like Ruth we should enter God's field and be willing to serve. Like Ruth, we should abandon ourselves to our glorious, heavenly "Boaz," and stay at His feet until morning.

Fuchsia Pickett, *The Prophetic Romance* (Lake Mary, FL: Charisma House, 1996), 54–58.

TWENTY-EIGHT

FINDING *the* STRENGTH *to* KEEP *on* GOING

by

Cathy Lechner

As THE CHILDREN OF ISRAEL REACHED THE BORDER of the land God promised them, they were directed to send twelve spies into the country. (See Numbers 13–14.) One man from each of the twelve tribes was chosen. They traveled for forty days, seeing everything and everyone in order to bring back a report to the people.

Joshua and Caleb were the only two who believed they should obey God and enter the Promised Land immediately. They tried to convince the people to act on faith, but the Israelites would not listen.

The ten spies who brought the bad report and caused the Israelites to grumble were immediately struck by a plague and died. They didn't even get a forty-year reprieve.

God is a merciful God. He tolerates our immaturity, but there comes a time when we must reach maturity in Christ. If we do not—if we don't fulfill our destiny and don't walk in the things the Spirit of God has for us—then He will give that destiny to someone else.

We often sing songs that ask God to melt us, mold us, break us, fill us—and what does God do? He puts us in situations that do just that. I can just see the angel when God is ready to melt us. He tells him to turn up the fire. It's so hot that the angel has to use tongs; then he applies the heat. And we begin to cry, "I bind that, I bind that!" All God is doing is what you asked Him to. He's burning off the old flesh. Then He can mold us into what He wants us to become.

It's painful. I would love to tell you that God will just take you all to Disney World and let you have a hilarious time, but that's not how it works.

When the children of Israel reached Canaan, the manna stopped appearing each morning. They had reached the land flowing with milk and honey. Was the milk flowing down in waterfalls off the mountaintops? No. Where was the milk? In the cow, of course.

"That's just great. Now I've got to put up with these flies and sit here and milk this cow." And how about the honey? "In the beehive? I thought it would just be there. I just know I'm going to get stung."

It's never the way we thought it was going to be, is it? It was always a lot easier in the tent. Just lift up the old flap while everyone is comfy in their sleeping bags, scrape in some manna, and feed the whole family.

It never ceases to amaze me how many precious believers are content living in the wilderness with only "manna" to sustain them. After a season, manna becomes boring and the children of Israel became discontent and wanted more. They tried to get God's attention by murmuring and whining.

It is still the same today. As long as our needs are met, we become complacent and our faith is never really challenged.

Three million Israelites complained while one man, Moses, prayed. God heard and moved because of that one man. Believe me, I know from experience that complaining gets you nowhere with God.

The Word says, "The Lord inhabits the praises of His people." Who is it that inhabits the complaining of His people? Whining brings the enemy into our situation while praising brings God into action in our situation.

If you have lost hope for your need, problem, or situation, the Lord has good news for you:

1. Return to the place of total surrender.

2. Begin to verbally praise and thank Him.

3. Think of your loving Father not only as your provider but also as your provision.

He is not only your bread for life; He is the Bread of Life!

Cathy Lechner, *I'm Trying to Sit at His Feet, but Who's Going to Cook Dinner?* (Lake Mary, FL: Charisma House, 1995), 146–149.

TWENTY-NINE

BREAK FREE FROM RELIGION

by
Kimberly Daniels

THE BIBLE WARNS BELIEVERS TO BE CAREFUL THAT THE light in them does not become darkness (Luke 11:35). Darkness descends when the light of the gospel is overshadowed by traditions handed down by men. In such cases, the Word of God is set aside, deprived of its authority and power.

How can we avoid letting our light become darkness? By steering clear of religious traps! The Greek word for "darkness" is *skotos*, which means shadiness or obscurity. The bondage of tradition is part of the shadiness that shuts out the light of the gospel in us.

Understand, tradition in itself is not a bad thing. The problem arises when church people attempt to make their generational rules and regulations equal to the Word of God. When they pass down their religious traditions, social customs, and belief systems by mouth or by practice, without validating their origin or explaining their purpose, they breed shadiness and darkness.

Their doctrines and traditions become like cement that has

settled. The church is bound, with no room for any person, place, or thing that doesn't fit with what's already there.

The Pharisees were bound by their customs and traditions. Jesus called them hypocrites! In Matthew 23:13, He told them, "You shut up the kingdom of heaven against men; for you neither go in yourselves, nor do you allow those who are entering to go in" (NKJV).

Two verses later He said, "You travel land and sea to win one proselyte [or convert], and when he is won, you make him twice as much a son of hell as yourselves" (v. 15, NKJV). Apparently there is a demonic double portion that operates through this religious, anti-evangelistic spirit!

As the return of Jesus draws closer, you would think that the hearts of God's people would grow closer to Him. The apostle Paul knew differently. In 2 Timothy 3:1–7, Paul spoke about the apostasy, or the falling away from the truth. He listed numerous spirits that would be operating in church people in the last days.

These people, Paul said, would have "a form of godliness" (v. 5, NKJV). The Greek word for "form" is *morphosis*, which means "an appearance." There are fashions in the church world today that put pressure on Christians to present a certain appearance, to be religiously "in vogue." In many churches, if a ministry gift isn't wrapped in the right package, it's not considered religiously correct.

But Romans 12:1 shows us how we must present ourselves as believers. We must not have a "form of godliness" that is worldly in nature. We must not be conformed to the world but transformed!

The Greek word for "transformed" is related to our English word *metamorphosis*, which means "to change appearance." Only as we are changed in appearance will people see the light of the gospel in us and "come in."

Religious spirits of tradition work to keep a church from being transformed. They block the light necessary to draw in new converts. When we finally deal with frivolous church customs and traditions, great evangelism will begin to take place!

Thankfully, there is hope. First Peter 1:18 tells us that we have been "redeemed...from [the] aimless conduct received by tradition" (NKJV) from our forefathers. We have been redeemed! Through the power of God's Spirit, we can reject dark, aimless, and harmful traditions that are based on man-made doctrines and not on the Word of God.

Will it be easy? No, but the reward will be great. It was for me!

My prayer is that God will anoint and empower you to see the religious spirits of tradition standing in the doorway of your calling. Don't let your light become darkness! Reject these religious spirits, and make a path for the next generation to see the light and come in.

Kimberly Daniels, "Break Free From Religion," *SpiritLed Woman*, June/July 2006, 34–37.

THIRTY

MIDLIFE MOMENTS
WITH *the* MASTER

by
Janet Maccaro

A MELTDOWN THAT OCCURS AT MIDLIFE LEADS TO SELF-examination. It forces us to take a deeper look at our lives. Old rooted beliefs are unearthed and discarded. And, maybe for the very first time, unbelief is challenged or replaced with faith.

> We know that all things work together for good to those who love God, to those who are the called according to His purpose.
>
> —Romans 8:28, NKJV

If you have experienced a meltdown, be encouraged! Midlife meltdowns have a positive side made up of two very strong beliefs. First, you must have faith that God has a plan and purpose for your life. Second, you must have faith that God will work your midlife trials out for your ultimate good, regardless of how your situation may look.

You still need to take care of your physical body, devote quality time to relationships, and focus on all of the other aspects of midlife that need attention, however. This simply means that you can rest in the fact that even though midlife is a challenge to us, testing our armor and sometimes leaving us grappling with the very meaning of our existence, we need not view it from a defeated perspective. Midlife trials can grow us, forming us into stronger, wiser, better people. It is all in how you perceive it.

Why do some people sail through midlife virtually unscathed, while others are weighed down with financial worries, relationship trouble, illness, and more? The answer could be that we may be harboring unforgiveness, bitterness, anger, and resentment buried deep within that needs to be purged. This in turn leads to self-examination.

Many times our loudest wake-up call comes at midlife in the form of a meltdown. Like a pitcher of ice water poured on our midlife morning face, God can use a meltdown to get our undivided attention. It is at midlife that we are brought to a place where we need to change our behavior or beliefs. At midlife we are forced to get back to the real person God meant us to be. Midlife trials have a way of stripping us completely of pride, ego, materialism, and anything that is driving us away from our full potential.

By the time we reach midlife, over half of our time on Earth is over. Midlife is the time for us to rekindle or strengthen our relationship with God. Sometimes it takes a "midlife crucifixion" for us to run back to our Father. Midlife transformations can leave you fully transformed, fully filled with God's love and presence, and fully ready to live eternally.

It is important to remember that while we are here on Earth we are spiritual beings having a human experience. Midlife can reaffirm this fact because it can compel us to embrace our spirituality. This is supernatural restoration by the grace of God. It is not a religion; it is a regeneration. When it occurs, it is radical. It is passionate. It is truth. Your spirit will know and recognize this. It is like coming home. When this occurs, especially during midlife and all of its trials, you will enjoy and take comfort in the fact that you will have fellowship with God.

And fellowship with God equals true happiness. Many great men before us confessed that without God, life was meaningless. With Him, the possibilities were endless. Empires were conquered and wars won when, to the natural mind, such outcomes seemed like impossibilities. These great men of old knew from whence their help came.

Midlife meltdown does happen. But forewarned is forearmed. Use your midlife experiences as catalysts for midlife transformation. Let your motto for midlife be: "Not my will, but Your will be done."

Janet Maccaro, *Midlife Meltdown* (Lake Mary, FL: Siloam, 2004), 179–181.

SECTION THREE

EXPERIENCING LIFE
WITH OTHERS

THIRTY-ONE

CHOOSING *for* LIFE:
A DUET SUNG WITH LOVE

by

Diana Hagee

GOD TELLS US IN HIS WORD TO CHOOSE FOR LIFE AND not for death; blessing and not for the curse. Make a conscious choice to choose for success of your marriage. Make a proclamation before the Lord and your spouse as you do so.

To choose for the success of your marriage, you must take certain steps that will enable you to have the relationship you desire with your spouse as you walk hand in hand in life.

First, you must stay connected to the Creator who fashioned you in His image. The Book of Psalms promises that God is near to all who call on Him in truth. When you call on the name of God, hope enters your speech, your mind, and your heart. Where there is life, there is hope. Jesus Christ is the living water and the blessed hope.

Second, you must repent before God, whom you have offended. Every time you have shown insult, anger, or disdain for your spouse, you have shown it to God. The act of repentance tells the Lord you have recognized your sin, have shown remorse, and are ready to begin anew. Repentance is one of the greatest acts of obedience you will ever commit.

Choose to keep the covenant. You must make a decision to stay married to your spouse for the rest of your life. Your spouse may have hurt you, but learn to forgive, for those who forgive will be forgiven. You must choose to love your spouse second only to Christ, your Savior. In order to be committed to any relationship, you must choose to love. Loving as Christ loves is the greatest accomplishment you can attain.

Choose today to show, without reservation, the love that God has put into your heart for your spouse. The desire you have for romance must be within the confines of the holy sacrament of matrimony. Any temptation to take this desire outside of marriage is an evil inclination that will deceive you and demand instant gratification no matter what the cost.

Know that God has a great plan for your marriage. Together you will serve Him in the path He has chosen for you. He takes the most painful situations in our lives and makes them testimonials to His power. We are given challenges so that we can learn to overcome—not to give in.

God always has a greater plan. As you and your spouse wait on Him to reveal to you His plan, determine to be patient, learn to persevere, and always trust in a God who will never disappoint you. These choices will change your life forever.

Pray these words:

> *Today we choose to live our lives for You, Father, and to hear Your voice, obey Your commandments, and wait on Your blessings.*

Diana Hagee, *What Every Woman Wants in a Man* (Lake Mary, FL: Charisma House, 2005), 148–149.

THIRTY-TWO

ROMANCING MY MAN

by
Diana Hagee

ROMANCE IS SO MUCH MORE THAN JUST SEXUAL INTI-macy. Romance lasts. Romance generates a love so deep that if sex were not possible for whatever reason, love would still grow. Romantic affection creates the necessary environment for a good marriage, and sex is one of the main events. Romance is precious.

My husband and I sat together in our bedroom and created the following seven romantic things a man and a woman can do for one another to generate romance in their marriage. Consider these seven ways to romance your husband.

1. Tell him you love him.

Men want to know they are loved. Love notes in his brief-case, travel bag, or clothes drawer does wonders to confirm your love for him. Sign your note with a kiss, wearing his favorite color lipstick, and spray your perfume on it! An e-mail with a scripture of blessing over your husband, along with a PS that says "I love you," will bring a smile to his heart. Men want to know they are loved.

2. Praise him.

Encouragement is so important. To tell your husband you are proud of him does more for him than you know. A wife's support of her husband contributes more to his success than any other factor. Men want to know they are important; don't take them for granted.

3. Prepare a special meal for him.

Yes, I really did write that. No, I wasn't forced. When a wife prepares a special meal for her husband, he is aware of the time she put forth in creating it. She has let him know he is important enough to her that she is willing to sacrifice her time and effort to make this loving gesture. Men like to be pampered.

4. Give him gifts.

How do you feel when your husband buys a present for you? You feel like a queen with all the wealth of the world. Give gifts to your husband too. The gift doesn't have to be expensive. The fact that you thought of it with him in mind will be more than sufficient. Men love presents.

5. Surprise him.

There are so many ways to create romance with surprises. What about a picnic? Date nights make for great surprises. Occasionally I call my husband and ask him if he would like to have an exciting date for the evening. I make arrangements for dinner and a movie. Sometimes I put his favorite chocolate on his pillow so he can find it when he prepares for bed. The anticipation that surprises create is so essential for romance. Men love surprises.

6. The power of your touch

One of the most beautiful pictures of romance I have ever seen is one I witness every Sunday morning at Cornerstone Church. On the front row center of the second section sit a wonderful man and his precious wife. They are in their late eighties. They sit so close to each other you couldn't get a sheet of paper between them. Every Sunday they hold each other's hand. These two wrinkled and gnarled hands are clasped tightly, and the other two hands are raised in praise and worship to the Lord. What a statement they make! The message of romance they send every Sunday is a memorial to the love they have for each other and the love they have for God. Men love hugs and kisses.

7. Loyalty

Remember the sacred vows you made. They are your word and your bond. Proverbs 31 describes the perfect woman as being one in whom "her husband safely trusts" (v. 11, NKJV). Trust is the fabric of every human connection. Trust is the cornerstone of your marriage relationship. There is nothing more special for a man than to know that the woman he loves can be trusted and that she will never bring him heartache.

Diana Hagee, *What Every Woman Wants in a Man* (Lake Mary, FL: Charisma House, 2005), 125–131.

THIRTY-THREE

WORDS *of* LOVE *and* PRAISE

by
Babbie Mason

IF YOU'RE MARRIED, YOU KNOW THE DIFFERENCE A WORD, spoken or unspoken, can make. There's plenty in the Bible that tells us we should be careful with words. In Proverbs, for example: "A word fitly spoken is like apples of gold in settings of silver" (Prov. 25:11, NKJV).

By the seventh year of our marriage, the honeymoon period was over. Charles and I, like many other couples, had learned to bicker and find fault with each other constantly. The love was still there, but often our words didn't match up with it. We began to antagonize one another a lot—and we did it with words.

We could have periods of peace and even discuss why were weren't getting along. Then Charles would say something hurtful or insensitive to me, and I'd use my extensive vocabulary to belittle him.

This unproductive behavior went on for years. Still, as

angry as we were at times, we were determined to make our marriage work. By the grace of God we kept on keeping on. But we still remained largely unaware of the huge impact our words, for better or worse, had on our happiness.

I don't know when the healing began, but I know that through much prayer, God gave me the grace to accept my husband exactly as he is—and God gave Charles the grace to accept me. Our personality differences are many, but our marriage has become stronger because of them. The fact that we are opposites has proven to be our strength.

Charles meets me head-on, seeing most issues in black and white. I always have to weigh the different shades of things. Charles weighs an issue with his head; I weigh it with my heart. Now we can consider an issue from both standpoints and together work out the best way to handle things.

Because women are so verbal, it's easy to talk rings around the man we love, forcing his verbal skills to dry up even more! And if he mispronounces words, as Charles sometimes does, and we continually correct him, no wonder some of us feel starved for sweet talk from our man.

Heaven only knows how many words from my husband's mouth had to be corrected by this schoolteacher wife before God corrected me for my own mispronunciation—for my own good. What's more, He corrected me publicly, at the height of a successful concert, just prior to my closing song one evening.

God used that incident to humble me and allow me to see that I too am capable of mispronouncing a word now and then. I well remember my discomfort and the sting of being "corrected." That night I learned that I don't need to correct others, but rather to watch my own words, each one of them, seeking to make not perfection but love, tenderness, kindness, healing, and encouragement my goal.

Verbal women, unite! Let's put some words of love and praise out there in our hurting and abusive world!

Babbie Mason, *Treasures of Heaven in the Stuff of Earth* (Lake Mary, FL: Charisma House, 2000), 71–74.

THIRTY-FOUR

A SYMPHONY of SUBMISSION SECRETS

by
Diana Hagee

THERE ARE SOME SUBMISSION SECRETS I WANT TO SHARE with you in order to give you a fair opportunity to successfully accomplish this God-ordained mandate. As you learn to obey God's instruction to be submissive to your husband, you can help him to become an effective and godly leader. The following ten submission secrets will help you to do that:

1. Respect him. Show honor and reverence in your home and to your friends and family (1 Tim. 3:11).
2. Acknowledge his calling as the high priest of your home. Don't try to override his authority with your children in the spirit of Absalom (2 Sam. 15:4).
3. Respond to his leadership. Don't tell him you will follow him and then do your own thing. You may deceive your husband for a season, but you won't fool the Lord for a second (Heb. 4:12).

4. Praise him. Women do not realize that a man needs praise just as often as a woman needs it. Praise your husband for providing for your home and family and for leading you in the ways of the Lord (Eph. 5:33).

5. Be unified with him in purpose and in will. When you come together as one in your goals and your supplications, God acknowledges your unity, and He grants your petitions (Amos 3:3).

6. Be his helpmate. Don't compete with your husband. Learn to complement him (Gen. 2:19).

7. Listen to him. Don't be the mouth of the body when God is calling you to be the ear and heart of the body (Prov. 4:4).

8. Pray with him and for him. It is so important that God hear your petitions for your husband. Cover him in prayer daily, praying that discernment and wisdom will guide him (Eph. 6:18).

9. Bless him. I try to bless my husband every day before he leaves our home. There is a battlefield outside of the doors of our home, and he needs all the help he can get. The power of the blessing provides a blanket of protection and favor (Num. 6:24–27).

10. Be thankful for him. So many women do not realize the gift her husband truly is until they lose him. Thank the Lord every day for your husband, and call out the traits that God wants in him to be the man He has destined him to be (1 Cor. 1:4–8).

Diana Hagee, *What Every Woman Wants in a Man* (Lake Mary, FL: Charisma House, 2005), 28–30.

THIRTY-FIVE

WHO IS IT THAT REALLY NEEDS *to* CHANGE?

by
Diana Hagee

ARE YOU ONE OF THE WOMEN WHO BELIEVE THAT IF only your husband would make some changes and become more like what you believe he should be, then life would be just about perfect? Maybe you need to learn a lesson I had to learn early in my marriage.

I have come to the conclusion that men are truly different. The adage says, "Thank God for the difference!" As women, it is important to identify the differences and acknowledge that God created most of these differences. We have no business changing that which God has ordained.

When I was newly married, I attended a Bible study taught by an older lady in the church. She told the young group of women that if we wanted to change certain characteristics in our husbands, we should pray. Eventually, God would make the changes we desired.

I was sure what she was saying had to be right on target—after all, she was an older woman! I went directly home, made my "Change Order," and submitted it to God.

I put my wish list in my Bible and prayed over it every day. "Lord, make my husband more spontaneous and less methodical. Make him more flexible and less rigid. Make him want to smell the roses and not trample over them."

One morning, the answer came. As I was praying, a thought came to my mind: "Today you will receive the man you have been praying for. I will make the changes in him you have requested." I knew it was God. I was excited. I thought, "That wasn't difficult at all!" As I was celebrating my answered prayer, another thought came just as unexpectedly as the first. It seemed God wasn't finished: "Today, I will give you the husband you want—but then I can no longer use him."

My celebration turned to spontaneous humility. I began to weep. I knelt on the floor and asked God to forgive me. My husband no longer used of God? I could hardly stand it! "Because of me? Please, Lord, no!" I prayed fervently. After my time of repentance was complete, the sweet presence of the Holy Spirit comforted me as He began to show me how He used the traits He put in my husband for His purposes.

The methodical approach he has for life is what God molds into the discipline needed for the hours of study and preparation of the Word of God. It enables my husband to present his message to the sheep of His pasture every Sunday. His rigid stance is the strength he must draw from when standing on the uncompromising message of the gospel of Jesus Christ. The determination that drives him is the tenacity the Creator put in him to fight injustice and stand for good, no matter what the cost. I wanted to change that which the Creator put into him for His purpose. I was the one who needed to change.

Diana Hagee, *What Every Woman Wants in a Man* (Lake Mary, FL: Charisma House, 2005), 93–94.

THIRTY-SIX

The POWER *of* HARMONIOUS COMMUNICATION

by

Diana Hagee

WOMEN OFTEN FALSELY ACCUSE MEN OF NOT LISTENING. We know they can hear us all right—they are just not paying attention. Actually, this is a gift. A man can follow the moves of a graceful quarterback on the turf while watching TV or track the path of a little white ball on the green until it falls in a shallow hole, all the while nodding and occasionally delivering a *hmm* while his wife is having a passionate, cathartic, one-sided conversation with him.

We want our husbands to communicate with us in the same way we communicate with other women. They can't. Bill Cosby said, "Women don't want to hear what you [men] think. Women want to hear what they think, in a deeper voice." Men want women to be content with the quality of communication they have with other men. We won't be.

I want to share with you the best form of communication you will ever experience with your spouse. It is the communication you have in prayer with each other and with God. The Lord uses communication to maintain a lifeline to His people. He uses several forms of communication. One is His written Word. Another is His voice, which is manifested through our conscience. He speaks to us through His people, who are the hands and feet of the living God. We, in turn, communicate to our Father in supplication, in praise, and in worship. Without participation in these forms of communication, the Christian will become distant from God, and his soul will soon dry and wither.

When we come to Him united, in one accord, as husband and wife, and lay our needs at His altar, our Lord makes a promise to us. Jesus is the promise keeper of all promise keepers.

> Again I tell you, if two of you on earth agree (harmonize together, make a symphony together) about whatever [anything and everything] they may ask, it will come to pass and be done for them by My Father in heaven.
> —Matthew 18:19, AMP

Can you imagine? Anything and everything! The operative words in this promise are "agree," "harmonize," and "symphony." What beautiful music we must make in the heavens when we pray together with our spouses in unity.

Find a private time and place for prayer. Satan will make sure that the phone will ring, your children will scream for you, or the doorbell will ring. My husband and I like to have our prayer time while we walk. We are away from intrusions and able to call on the Lord in freedom. I am sure you and your husband can find a place and time on which you can agree.

Make a prayer list. Learn to pray in agreement, not in competition. There is no sweeter sound in the heavens than the sound of a husband and wife in harmony before the throne of God. There is nothing more powerful.

The more this divine communication occurs, the more you will want to talk to each other about other things. You will find that the "things" you speak about with your spouse will not include gossip or tale bearing. Your conversation will concentrate on the petitions that you put before the Lord and the testimonies associated with those prayers. With your husband you will share the dreams and aspirations each of you has as together you come into agreement. Your children will know that when Mom and Dad pray, things happen. This teaching is far greater than any book or class you will ever enroll them in. Without communication, your marriage will wither and dry, just like the soul when it has no time with God.

Diana Hagee, *What Every Woman Wants in a Man* (Lake Mary, FL: Charisma House, 2005), 93–94, 100–101.

THIRTY-SEVEN

GOD'S COUNTRY TUNE: TAKE THIS MARRIAGE *and* FIX IT!

by

Linda S. Mintle

MANY COUPLES STAGGER TO A SAD MOMENT IN THEIR relationship when it feels that nothing can save the marriage. They either feel utter contempt for their partner, or they are convinced that the only solution for emotional health is divorce.

They have given up. The future looks grim unless there is drastic change. Without hopeful signs of change, separation and divorce become ultimate solutions. They are tired of fighting. There is too much bad history to overcome, or they can no longer tolerate the spouse's behavior. They are "out of love," have "grown apart," or "are too different." Marriage was a mistake, came too soon, was chosen out of desperation, or became too confining. Whatever the reason, the belief is, "It's just too late to make this work."

This may be reality if you look only at the circumstances and relationship issues. But there is more to consider. And that is where hope springs eternal. Without hope, troubled marriages face disaster.

When you feel that you are at the end of the road and the next stop is divorce, remember who your real enemy is. It may seem that it's your spouse. He may be doing things that are hurtful, rejecting, and angry. But the real enemy behind divorce is not a person. There is a bigger force trying to destroy what God has put together. It is a force of darkness. It is real and operates in an invisible world that exists all around us. You are about to do battle with a spiritual enemy.

How do you begin to war against the force behind all the unhappiness? First, believe there are principalities and powers operating against you. Second, clean up your act. Line up your thinking with God's. Get your behavior in line with godly living. Then begin to fill yourself up with the Word of God and His promises. Say them, rehearse them, and claim them as your own. Your mouth has the power of life and death, according to the Bible. Confess life and new breath into your marriage. Confessing what God says about you and your situation brings new belief that it is true.

Next, do battle against those dark forces. Identify the spiritual roots of problems and attack them in the Spirit. For example, "I pray against that anger that is gripping my spouse. I have the authority to demand it go away in Jesus's name. I command it to go. Greater is He that is in me than he that is in the world. Anger, you have no authority in this house. I pray the peace of God over this place." Walk the floors, talk to God, take back what is yours by the authority given you in Jesus's name!

Even when you feel tired and defeated, remind yourself that it's not over until it's over. Command doubt to leave you. Rehearse God's track record in impossible situations. Enlist one or two fellow Christians who understand how to war against this enemy. Meet with them regularly for prayer. You also need to be under the mantle of an anointed pastoral staff that prays and intercedes on your family's behalf. Wrap up all your weariness and use it in prayer. "God, I am weak, but in my weakness You promised to be strong. Make me strong to fight. You have given me the power to defeat the enemy. I want to start using that power now."

Too many Christians are spiritual anorexics. They have access to a feast of power but restrict its use because they are ignorant of God's Word or mistakenly too afraid to move by His Spirit. Use the resources your good and trustworthy heavenly Father has given you to overcome lies and move in His power. You are sons and daughters of the King. Start claiming your inheritance.

Linda S. Mintle, *Divorce Proofing Your Marriage* (Lake Mary, FL: Siloam, 2001), 219–220, 227–228.

THIRTY-EIGHT

LET NOTHING TERRIFY YOU

by
Paula Sandford

THERE ARE MANY PASSAGES IN THE BIBLE THAT CALL YOU to live in a way that seems extremely difficult and often nearly impossible in the midst of a sinful generation. Not the least of these is 1 Peter 3:1–6, which encourages married women to live in a respectful relationship with their husbands.

The Amplified Bible translates verse 6 this way: "…if you do right and let nothing terrify you [not giving way to hysterical fears or letting anxieties unnerve you]." What anxieties are there to unnerve a woman? What is there to terrify her? Paul is not referring to a specific category of battered and abused wives. He is addressing married women in general.

What Do We Do With Fears and Feelings?

Part of learning to love your husband is learning to give each other space from time to time. It's healthy for you and your marital relationship. As a woman, learn to develop outside interests that are not dependent on her husband so that your strength is renewed when it's time to come together. If you're not married, you still need friends.

As women, our friendships with other women are vitally important. We need the fellowship of a few close friends with whom we can talk to, laugh, and cry, people with whom we share common interests and know how to enjoy life.

You will also benefit greatly from regular exercise, music, and good books. Take some time to hone a skill, whatever it may be—sewing, painting, crafts, writing. The ideal situation is for you to become grounded in the nurturing and supportive fellowship of a good, Bible-believing church. Use wisdom when scheduling your time out to avoid a conflict with your husband's need to be with you; otherwise he will feel like he's competing for your attention and become jealous.

So how do we avoid giving way to hysterical fears, not letting anxieties unnerve us? God's Word is clear:

> Cast your burden upon the LORD, and He will sustain you;
> He will never allow the righteous to be shaken.
> —Psalm 55:22, NAS

Your necessary righteous discipline is to cast your burden on the Lord when you first become aware of it, before it has the opportunity to take firm hold of you. Don't entertain it. Don't wallow in it. Don't feed it with resentment and bitterness. Acknowledge it, offer it to the Lord, release it, affirm your identity in Him, and go about your business.

Paula Sandford, *Healing for a Woman's Emotions* (Lake Mary, FL: Charisma House, 2007), 55.

THIRTY-NINE

SOMETIMES IT JUST TAKES
a LOVE LETTER

by

Babbie Mason

THERE'S A STORY MAKING THE ROUNDS THAT MAKES ME chuckle. It seems a young man and his female roommate invited his mother over for dinner.

Now the mother, suspicious of this male-female arrangement, felt extra concern as she watched her son relate to the pretty young thing. As she watched the two over the course of the evening, John's momma felt more and more certain she didn't like the situation.

"I know what you're thinking," her son told her, "but let me assure you that Julie and I are just roommates."

A week later, Julie asked John about a missing piece of her silver service. "Ever since your mother's visit, I can't seem to find that beautiful silver gravy ladle," she remarked. "You don't suppose she took it, do you?"

"I doubt it," John replied, "but I'll write a letter to Mom to make sure." His letter read:

Dear Mother,

I'm not saying you did take the gravy ladle from the house, and I'm not saying you did not take it. I am saying, however, that it has been missing since you came to dinner.

Love, John

Several days later, John received a reply from his mother. She wrote:

Dear Son,

I'm not saying you do sleep with Julie, and I'm not saying you do not. I am saying, however, that if she were sleeping in her own bed, she would have found the gravy ladle by now.

Love, Mom

Lesson of the day: don't lie to your mom.

Babbie Mason, *Treasures of Heaven in the Stuff of Earth* (Lake Mary, FL: Charisma House, 2000), 36–37.

FORTY

MENTORED *for* MOTHERHOOD *by* MY HEAVENLY FATHER

by

Paula Sandford

MOTHERHOOD HAS ALWAYS BEEN A TREMENDOUS PRIVI-lege (and responsibility) that brings, I believe, joys and rewards that far outweigh possible difficulties and sorrows. As a mother, you will never in any other circumstance have an opportunity to influence the life of another human being so profoundly as you do your own child.

There are things you can do to build strength into your child at every stage of development in his or her life. While your baby is in your womb, pray daily for protection and blessing. Your unborn child has the capacity to experience, receive, and respond. If you faithfully voice the prayers, it is God's job to make something happen.

Hold and tenderly rock your baby. Talk and sing to him or her. Babies comprehend much more with their sensitive little spirits than they do with their minds. Encourage your husband to participate in caring for the baby. If his arms are strong and gentle, the baby will begin to develop positive anticipation of the world away from you and security apart from you.

Take time to play with your child. Laugh with your child. As your son or daughter develops, read stories, work, and play together. Encourage, compliment, listen, teach with patience, and give appropriate hugs and kisses. Apply discipline consistently with love, never with condemnation.

Don't stifle your children's sense of adventure. As they become older and begin to venture into the neighborhood, pray for their protection, and let them go. Give older children room to grow. When you're tempted to give unsolicited advice, bite your tongue.

Be an example to your child on how to pray. Pray for the protection of your children at every level of their development. Especially when they are in their teens, stand with them in spiritual warfare against the forces of darkness in the world that would press in to threaten, seduce, attack, oppress, or push them in any way.

Travail for them in prayer as Paul spoke of in Galatians 4:19. You must not try to control them, or you will drive them away from you and from the Lord.

Trust God to care for them. As you begin to give your children more freedom to take responsibility for their own lives, trust God and the deposit of love and nurture that has been built into them. Or, if you know those virtues to be seriously lacking in their foundations, make a decision to trust God's redemptive power. God is still able to rescue His children, set them on the right course, and bring them into the glory He has prepared for them.

Paula Sandford, *Healing for a Woman's Emotions* (Lake Mary, FL: Charisma House, 2007), 179, 189, 193–194.

FORTY-ONE

GOD NURTURES *the* HEART *of* MY PRESCHOOLER

by
C. Hope Flinchbaugh

WHY IS IT THAT TWO- AND THREE-YEAR-OLDS DELIGHT IN stashing things in secret places? Everything from dirty diapers to unwanted vegetables rot in some dark hole until fumes from their decomposition send us scrambling to uncover last month's hidden sin.

With our two-year-old Judah, it has always been vitamins. She doesn't like the taste of them, so she stashes them in her secret hiding spots all over the house. One night her daddy gave her a vitamin and told her to take it. He sweetly and convincingly persuaded her to take it in her tiny hand. She's quite the daddy's girl, and she smiled reassuringly while he walked away into the kitchen. She watched him leave, and then, unaware that I was watching her, as quickly as her little legs would go, she scooted into her bedroom. After looking around to be sure no one was watching, she did a hook shot with that vitamin, ricocheting it off the wall as she threw it behind the dresser.

Pleased that it made the mark, she turned around and walked back out to the living room. I turned my head and howled, then composed myself and told my husband what happened. He made her dig it out and dust it off, and she ate it anyway.

She had that same expression on her face as she did when we first offered her Gerber vegetables. It was a "don't-feed-me-any-more-of-that-green-stuff" look where she turned her head sideways, buttoned up those lips, and, out of the corner of her eye, dared us to try to make her eat it.

Judah's vitamins fall out of her car seat when I pull the tray up; they've been found in her shoes, in the tissue box, between the couch cushions, and in the trash can. Not only does she hide vitamins, but she also enjoys hiding herself whenever she's called. I wondered if we'd ever break the "hiding habit." Where can a parent turn when a child continues misbehaving?

I kept thinking, "She's not getting as many Bible stories as the older two did. I need to read more of the Word to her."

So I took a shot at reading more Bible stories. I tried the one about Jesus feeding the five thousand (Judah would gladly give Jesus her fish and bread if it meant she didn't have to eat it), David and Goliath (I wonder if she imagined slinging vitamins instead of stones), and God creating the world.

Judah would impatiently listen to my story choice and always ask for the Jonah story. I was thinking, "Jonah?" Over and over I would read Jonah from two or three different storybooks she found. After about two weeks of Jonah, Judah looked up at me one day while we were on page five and said, "He hidin'."

Lights. More lights. A sonic boom.

HIDING! That's it! I suddenly felt transformed from "Super-bomb" to "Supermom!" I went for it!

"That's right. Jonah's hiding. Does God see Jonah?"

Judah nodded her little head. "Jonah should obey God. He shouldn't hide when God calls him."

Well, God ministered this story to Judah by His Holy Spirit. I didn't understand why she liked this particular story read to her over and over again. I was certainly tiring of Jonah. But God was ministering His life into my little girl, and when she showed me what that story meant to her, my trust in God soared.

And the vitamins? Well, she seems to be doing better, but let's just say I haven't cleaned behind her dresser for a while.

Whenever we call her, and Judah chooses to hide, all we have to do is say, "Could Jonah hide from God?" And eventually she crawls out of some dark hole grinning in obedient triumph. I love it! The Word works!

C. Hope Flinchbaugh, *Spiritually Parenting Your Preschooler* (Lake Mary, FL: Charisma House, 2003), 31–32.

FORTY-TWO

BLISSFUL BLENDING *at the* HAND *of* GOD

by

Joanne and Seth Webster

J ESUS HAD A STEPFATHER.

For all that is said in praise of the nuclear family, God's Word is full of stories about blended families, fractured families, stepfamilies, and horribly dysfunctional families—far more, in fact, than happily adjusted, biologically correct nuclear families, which we call normal. God sent His own Son to be part of a blended family. It appears that Joseph, the stepfather chosen for Jesus, was equal to the task and raised fine children of tremendous character without favoritism, even though one of them was indisputably perfect. Tough act for the other kids to follow!

Joseph, and even his wife, Mary, came from a long line of less-than-ideal families. Extended lifetimes, premature deaths, and ancient customs, including polygamy, all contributed to the blended families in the earthly genealogy of Christ—and in the genealogy of most of our heroes of faith. Think of Abraham, the patriarch of three religions. Abraham's father incorporated his grandson Lot into his family, and in the next generation, Abraham had a son with his wife Sarah's maid, keeping the blending going. Jacob, Moses, David, and Hannah all faced the challenge of surviving in blended families—the one they were raised in, the one they helped to create, or both.

God has a plan for your blended family. He loves you and cares for you, knows what you're up against, and understands your frustrations. In every situation, He already knows the way through it—even if you're the one who created the mess.

More than anything, we want to encourage you to press on no matter how difficult it sometimes seems. We are living proof that even if you make a few wrong turns, God will fulfill His promise to make beauty out of ashes. When the Israelites fled Egypt and came to the barrier of the Red Sea, the path they crossed on was there all along. It was just covered by a big sea that God had to move. Even if you get a little lost in your family, or face a big barrier, there is a way for you, a path to freedom. God is no "respecter of persons," so we are certain that what He did for us and for the Israelites, He is just as willing to do for you.

Joann and Seth Webster, *Can Stepfamilies Be Done Right?* (Lake Mary, FL: Charisma House, 2001), 4–6.

FORTY-THREE

RIGHT IS *a* SONG
SUNG *in* HARMONY

by

Joyce Meyer

THE BOOK OF JAMES TEACHES US THAT IF WE HAVE STRIFE in our lives and pride in our hearts, the pride will rise up and tell us we are walking in truth when we are actually deceived.

> But if you have bitter jealousy (envy) and contention (rivalry, selfish ambition) in your hearts, do not pride yourselves on it and thus be in defiance of and false to the Truth.
>
> —James 3:14, AMP

Have you ever been absolutely sure you were right about something? Your mind appeared to have a store of facts and details to prove you were right—but you ended up wrong. God uses experiences like that to show us how a prideful attitude opens the door and welcomes strife.

When Dave and I face such situations, God has enabled us to say, "I think I am right, but I may be wrong." It is absolutely amazing how many arguments we have avoided over the years by using that simple act of humility.

Believers are to avoid strife.

> And the servant of the Lord must not be quarrelsome (fighting and contending). Instead, he must be kindly to everyone and mild-tempered [preserving the bond of peace]; he must be a skilled and suitable teacher, patient and forbearing and willing to suffer wrong.
>
> —2 Timothy 2:24, AMP

A close look at the preceding verse gives us some insight into the "how to" of avoiding strife.

> But refuse (shut your mind against, have nothing to do with) trifling (ill-informed, unedifying, stupid) controversies over ignorant questionings, for you know that they foster strife and breed quarrels.
>
> —2 Timothy 2:23, AMP

I believe the verse is really saying this: "Stay out of conversations where no one knows what they are talking about and everybody is arguing over nothing." So often people argue over things that make no difference to anybody. Notice the word *trifling* in verse 23. It indicates things that are unimportant and make no difference when considered with things that are really important.

I have used this scripture a lot in various teachings, and people are always blessed by the Amplified Bible translation. In many situations nobody really knows what they are talking about—but everybody thinks they do. Pride wants desperately to look intelligent. The result is that the devil wins through strife.

Why do people strive so desperately to be right about things? Why is it so difficult to be wrong? Why is it so important to be right? Jesus was accused of wrongdoing regularly, yet never once did He attempt to defend Himself. He let people think He was wrong, and it did not disturb Him at all.

He could do so because He knew who He was. He did not have a problem with His self-image. He was not trying to prove anything. He trusted His heavenly Father to vindicate Him. For years I felt so bad about "who" I was. In order to feel confident at all, I had to think I was right all the time. I would argue to be right and go to great extremes to prove it.

Someone was always challenging me. I lived in frustration as I tried to convince everyone I knew what I was talking about. What a wonderful freedom it is not to have to do that any longer. Jesus came to set the captives free. People who argue over trifling issues just to prove they are right are definitely not free.

As my identity became rooted and grounded in Christ, I experienced more freedom in this area. My worth and value do not come from appearing right to others. They are found in the fact that Jesus loved me enough to die for me and bring me into a personal relationship with Him.

I gradually realized that great spiritual power is release through unity and harmony.

Joyce Meyer, *Life Without Strife* (Lake Mary, FL: Charisma House, 1995, 2000), 18–21.

FORTY-FOUR

FEAR IS MERELY FALSE EVIDENCE APPEARING REAL

by
Joyce L. Rodgers

Fear can enter our lives when we become appre-
hensive of the future. Women are especially susceptible
to this type of fear because we crave stability and security.
Marriage counselors agree that the No. 1 problem in marriages
is not incompatibility or even infidelity; rather, the greatest
problems arise from financial stress. In this time of economic
instability, it can be easy to fall victim to fear of our future
financial stability, and such fear can wreak havoc in our family
relationships. In the Sermon on the Mount, Jesus said that we
should take no thought for our lives; He was telling us not to
have fear about the material aspects of our lives. God provides
for the flowers of the earth and the birds of the air. How much
more will He care for us? (See Matthew 6:25–34.)

Fear can thrive in our hearts when we do not focus upon
the Giver of life and the promises contained in His Word.
Though terrible circumstances may arise and adverse situations

may come, we must not yield to fear; instead, we are to trust our God and respond to the problem in faith. The writer of Hebrews told of the response of Moses's parents to a frightening situation: "By faith Moses, when he was born, was hid three months of his parents, because they saw he was a proper child; and they were not afraid of the king's commandment" (Heb. 11:23). Moses's parents refused to give more credence to the commandment of Pharaoh than they did to the commandments of God.

When fear is allowed to maintain a stronghold in our lives, it is because we are putting more faith in the tangible than the intangible and more attention upon the problem than on the problem solver. Paul said, "For our light affliction, which is but for a moment, worketh for us a far more exceeding and eternal weight of glory" (2 Cor. 4:17). But this glory is only worked for us "while we look not at the things which are seen, but at the things which are not seen." Paul goes on to tell us why we should do this: "For the things which are seen are *temporal*; but the things which are not seen are *eternal*" (v. 18, emphasis added).

Although there are many tangible things that would try to overcome our hearts with fear, these things are not actually a threat to us! I heard a speaker once ascribe these words to the acronym of fear: "**F**alse **E**vidence **A**ppearing **R**eal." Ultimately, the things that we fear are in God's hands; they are "false evidence" that there is a problem that cannot be handled—false because God is totally in control of the situation!

Joyce L. Rodgers, *Fatal Distractions* (Lake Mary, FL: Charisma House, 2003), 167–168.

FORTY-FIVE

SPIRIT-*to*-SPIRIT RELATIONSHIPS
WITH OTHERS

by
Sheri Rose Shepherd

WE LIVE WITH IMPERFECT PEOPLE IN AN IMPERFECT world. Sharing the path of excellence with others can be extremely challenging because people can be very difficult to love. While we are all so different in our views, gifts, and ways, we do have one thing in common—our need for each other's love and acceptance. Sometimes, it seems like we can't live with each other, but we know we can't live without each other, either. I've heard many Christians say, "I love the ministry; I just don't like the people."

Some of us feel we could be the perfect mother if only we had that perfect child, or we could be perfect wives if we had perfect husbands. The truth is, we walk with imperfect people...just like us.

Have you ever thought about the fact that even if you don't like someone here on Earth, you might as well be nice to them because you might be neighbors in heaven? I always make sure

I'm extra nice to people I don't enjoy being around here on Earth. I figure hopefully that God will have their mansion in heaven built on the other side of the crystal sea from me!

To be emotionally healthy, we need to learn how to get along with each other. God gave us the Golden Rule of relationships thousands of years ago: "Do to others what you would have them do to you" (Matt. 7:12, NIV). If every one of us would live by this rule, we would live in harmony. As you walk along the path—with those you do like and those you don't—strive for excellence in your relationships by following the principles given below.

1. Respect each other's differences.
2. Create common ground.
3. Give others freedom to fail.
4. Tame your tongue.
5. Walk with character and credibility.
6. Walk in unity and love.

Love is the spiritual glue that connects us. Love is the reason God made us and the reason He sent His Son to redeem us. Love is also the fruit (the evidence) of God living inside us. People will know we belong to Him because of our love. This love is not a superficial love that we see so commonly around us, but it is God's definition of love...a spiritual love.

We can know many people and still feel very lonely in this world, in the church, or even in a marriage. Loneliness is cured when we learn to develop spirit-to-spirit relationships with each other.

Sheri Rose Shepherd, *Fit for Excellence!* (Lake Mary, FL: Charisma House, 2004), 131–140.

FORTY-SIX

EXPECT OPPOSITION

by
Judy Jacobs

THERE WILL ALWAYS BE AN OPPOSITION TO YOUR MISSION. Whenever you step out and begin to walk in obedience to God, there is going to be some kind of opposition from the devil. As soon as Jesus was baptized by John, He had to face the temptation in the wilderness. (See Matthew 4:1; Mark 1:12; Luke 4:1.)

Your opposition and adversity will take different forms at different times. Today, you may be facing a health problem. Last year, you may have been in a financial bind. Two years ago, perhaps you lost your job. Later on, you might have a lot of trouble with your teenager or conflict in your marriage or a difficult relationship with someone on the job. Sometimes your opposition is discouragement, sleepless nights, or the stress of having too much to do.

God never promised that you were going to float along on this journey of life, smelling roses and never having another problem from the day you were saved. He did promise that He will be with you (Isa. 43:2).

Get it through your head that trials, tests, and all kinds of difficulties are inevitable. God will allow as many of them as you can handle, and He always knows how much you can handle. Your part is to decide now that you are going all the way with Him, regardless of how much it hurts. You can be sure that He will train you and strengthen you every step of the way, because He wants you to be able to take every step in 100 percent faith.

Always remember that the devil brings temptations, but God brings tests. It's all for your benefit. It's all for your growth. The devil brings temptations to drive you away from God, but your God will help you resist them, and He will manage to convert those temptations into soul strengtheners. They become opportunities for your growth. God brings you into tests and trials, and they may seem counterproductive at first. But He's doing it because He loves you, so you can be pruned and shaped as you grow closer to Him.

Paul said it like this:

> We had the sentence of death in ourselves, that we should not trust in ourselves, but in God which raiseth the dead: Who delivered us from so great a death, and doth deliver: in whom we trust that he will yet deliver us.
>
> —2 Corinthians 1:9–10

Even if you may feel like you are facing death right now, Paul wanted you to know that if you just keep standing, He will deliver!

Judy Jacobs, *Stand Strong* (Lake Mary, FL: Charisma House, 2007), 79–80.

FORTY-SEVEN

MAKING FORGIVENESS *a* LIFESTYLE

by
Joyce Meyer

I LIVED FAR TOO LONG BEHIND WALLS I HAD BUILT TO protect myself from emotional pain because I was determined not to give anyone a chance to hurt me a second time.

I was no longer being abused, but I held the abuse in my heart, and it continued to cause pain in my life because I refused to trust God to vindicate me. It took many years for me to realize that I could not love anyone as long as I kept myself prisoner behind the walls of unforgiveness. I also had to learn that I really could not love and be loved until I was willing to take a chance on being hurt. Love hurts sometimes, but it also heals. It is the only force that will override hatred, anger, and unforgiveness. It is the only force that can heal broken or troubled relationships.

The world is filled with hurt and hurting people, and my experience has been that hurting people hurt others. The devil works overtime among God's people to bring offense, strife, and disharmony, but we can override his attempts to sow hatred, bitterness, anger, and unforgiveness. We can be quick to forgive.

Forgiveness closes the door to Satan's attack so that he cannot gain a foothold that might eventually become a stronghold. It can prevent or end strife in our relationships with others. No wonder Scripture tells us over and over that we are to forgive those who hurt or offend us.

> Be gentle and forbearing with one another and, if one has a difference (a grievance or complaint) against another, readily pardoning each other; even as the Lord has [freely] forgiven you, so must you also [forgive].
> —Colossians 3:13, AMP

When you and I refuse to forgive other people, we open a door for the devil to torment us. We lose our freedom—the glorious freedom that God intended us to have as we follow His ways. God is love. He is also merciful, kind, forgiving, and slow to anger. We often desire His power and blessings without wanting the lifestyle that goes with those things. Forgiveness must become a lifestyle.

We are to forgive people who ask our forgiveness, even when we are not aware that they have wronged us, because our forgiveness frees them to be at peace. For example, at times people have asked me to forgive them for not liking me or for speaking unkindly about me. I wasn't even aware of their problem. It was not hurting me—it was hurting them. I gladly forgave them because I wanted them to be free.

We are also to forgive people who do not ask our forgiveness, whether because they did not intend to offend us and do not know they did or because they are not repentant. Either way, forgiveness frees us from harboring bitterness and anger in our hearts. It releases us.

If you think you have offended someone, go the extra mile and simply say, "If I have offended you, I apologize." Then, if you discover that they indeed were offended, simply ask them to forgive you. The power of the words, "Please forgive me," is amazing! Should the individual refuse to forgive you, at least you have done your part and can dwell in peace.

Joyce Meyer, *Conflict Free Living* (Lake Mary, FL: Charisma House, 2008), 97–98, 100–101.

FORTY-EIGHT

MOTIVATED *by* LOVE *to* SERVE GOD *and* OTHERS

by

Fuchsia Pickett

THERE IS NO GREATER CALL TO THE WOMAN OF GOD than to live her life by demonstrating her love for God and her family by exhibiting the characteristics of a servant. Responding to the call to servanthood involves scrutinizing the attitudes and motivations that form the basis of our character. A true servant will be motivated by love. As you serve God and your family from your heart of love, you will exhibit these three characteristics of a servant.

1. Joy

Joy is the desired attitude of a servant. "The joy of the LORD is your strength" (Neh. 8:10). According to Dr. David Schoch, that verse literally reads, "The joy we experience in serving God gives us back our strength."* God's genuine approval of our

---

* *Matthew Henry's Commentary on the Whole Bible*, New Modern Edition, Electronic Database (Hendrickson Publishers, Inc., 1991).

service becomes strength for us to serve. A servant does each task joyfully. He doesn't stop working five minutes early, deciding not to start something else because it's quitting time. Neither is his attitude dependent upon his circumstances always being pleasant. It is written of Jesus, "Who for the joy that was set before him endured the cross" (Heb. 12:2). Jesus's suffering did not destroy His joy. A servant can endure great difficulty because he is convinced that his greatest privilege on earth is to serve God.

I loved my earthly daddy so much that it was a delight for me to serve him. I was delighted when he asked me, instead of my mother, to get his coffee. When he asked me to make him some cornbread, do you think I felt it was belittling? I practiced and practiced, dumping out one pan of cornbread after another until I could be sure I had made some that would please my daddy. It was my joy to serve him. If I could experience that joy in serving my earthly daddy, how much more should I rejoice in serving my heavenly Father? I am a daughter of God, and it is a supreme joy to serve Him. When we live as true servants, our service brings us pleasure; we don't complain over any menial task.

2. Faithfulness

Faithfulness further characterizes the servant heart. A servant is a faithful steward or overseer. A steward takes care of something that belongs to another person until that one can return to take care of it. As an overseer, he does not require the master to write out all the instructions, but is able to take on responsibility within a certain latitude. A servant develops as he works in an area, exploring its needs and responding to them. Every Christian has been given stewardship of a treasure within, that is, of the life of Jesus that God has invested in us. We are responsible to allow the character of Christ to be developed in us as we yield to the Holy Spirit's conviction and prompting, showing us where we need to be changed. We will not be rewarded for our educational degrees or our personal excellence, but for our faithful obedience as servants.

Our greatest commendation will be for God to say to us, "Well done, thou good and faithful servant" (Matt. 25:21). He does not commend the preacher, apostle, or minister—He commends the servant. Whether or not we have succeeded in man's eyes, if we earn God's commendation we have truly succeeded in life.

3. Humility

If joy is our attitude and faithfulness our measure of love, we can describe humility as the demeanor of our servant heart.

May God help us to leave the mark of one who picks up the towel and washes the feet of others. Humility is a beautiful attribute of the servant heart. Without humility there is no true servanthood. God is calling for servants who will be filled with the fruit of the Holy Spirit. He is not seeking those who desire honor and recognition, but those who serve Him because they love Him supremely.

Fuchsia Pickett, *God's Purpose for You* (Lake Mary, FL: Charisma House, 2003), 58–65.